# God Loves You

**Jean Khoury**

God Loves You

# Tables of Contents

Introduction _____ 5

Does God Love Us Always? _____ 7

Where Is Your Heart? _____ 17

God's Overwhelming Love For Us _____ 23

Jesus' Embrace On The Cross _____ 33

God Wants To Love Us _____ 37

The Revelation Of God's Love _____ 43

The Hidden Verses _____ 53

The Goal Of Our Life Is Union With Christ _____ 69

God Is Much Better Than You Believe _____ 81

Christ The Groom, What Does It Mean? _____ 85

The Act Of Oblation _____ 97

Therese's Copernican Revolution _____ 117

# Introduction

"Jesus looked at him and loved him." (Mk 10:21). We can easily overlook this passage. We think that it is not for us.
Who understands the extent of Jesus' love for each one of us?
How many people know that Jesus' love is the starting point of Christianity? The starting point of our day? The starting point of our prayer? He always has the initiative… always.
He searches for us much more than we search for Him, his Thirst to give himself to us is infinite and his Love is unconditional.

For many reasons we tend to forget his Love, doubt it and not open ourselves to His Love. This book is meant to strengthen our faith in Jesus' unconditional love. It closely follows the Scriptures.

My wish is that it could lead us to practise "contemplative prayer" on a daily basis. (See the important book indicated at the end of this book.)

Meditating these texts, reading the Scriptures with eyes that see and ears that hear is vital for us. We all need to receive Jesus' Love and to receive it, we need to be sure and convinced about it. This is the goal of this book. A first step, or a much-needed reminder, which opens our heart to receive Jesus' Love.

**Jean Khoury**

London, Christmas 2023

**Note:** One can find these chapters on this site: www.schoolofmary.org, please don't hesitate to check this site for more and share with others this important truth.

# Does God Love Us Always?

**Question:** If God creates a "new man" in me and the old man has to go completely, what is it that God loves in me then? If I am "made in his image and likeness" and "he has called me by my name", what is it in me that He loves? Does He only love the capacity to be like Him? Does He love us as far as we do His will, are transformed into Him and live His life and therefore our Ego has to go? Do you see the question, psychologically? If we need to be transformed into Him does the fact that "I am" mean anything?

The Prodigal Son and His Father

## Answer:

### Is the Old Man Different from Our Self?

The real meaning of the expression "Old Man" encompasses a way of acting and its deep roots in us. "Purification" and transformation into God does not imply the cancellation of our being.

It seems that to "go completely" from one state to the other means throwing out the baby with the dirty water. We must avoid this, please. We need to properly understand what the expression "Old Man" alludes to. The "old man" concerns behaviour rather than being – certainly not all of our being. It most certainly does not impinge on the self, but on our way of acting. We, therefore, should distinguish between on one hand our behaviour, acts, choices and, on the other hand, our being, our soul, spirit, the faculties of our soul, and our self.

There is a definite difference between a faculty in our soul (mind, will) and the use we make of this faculty. Hence, while it is true to say God loves each one of us, we can all agree that He doesn't love our sins! But, still, after sinning He still loves us – for who we are, not for this or that act. He hopes also that we can change. He wants us close to Him. He enjoys our presence. He desires even more – He wants to be united to us. When we say that the Old Man has to go, it doesn't mean that this happens in a mechanical way, like pressing "delete" and saying: "let us re-create from scratch". No. God doesn't re-create us from scratch. He needs us, from the first day, He needs our full collaboration, given freely... willingly. This is why St. Augustine says: God created us without our consent, but He won't save us without our consent. Our own salvation, realised on God's side, by Jesus on the Cross, cannot be fully received, enacted, to transform us, without our consent being given, at each step! It is not accomplished by one act but through a multitude of acts, coming from our free will.

In this sense, He cannot realise his salvation in us (realised first on the Cross), without us. God needs us!!

So, returning to the question, it is fair to say that "sin" and "grace" don't cancel out our being. They are the result, the fruits of our being, they give a colour and a shape to our being, but still they are not our being. We are something different, bigger, exceedingly bigger. The biggest sin is infinitely smaller than each one of us is in His eyes.

Spiritual authors often take the following verse from St. John out of context and apply it to the "Old Man" and the "New Man": "He must increase, I must decrease" (John 3:30). This verse is normally said by St. John the Baptist when talking about his mission. We can accept with tolerance the deviation in meaning. However, in order to understand better the meaning of Old Man vs New Man, it is better to re-read what St. Paul says in the following texts: Romans 13:12ss, Eph 4:13-27. See also: Rm 7:7-23); 2 Cor 4:16-17 ; Eph 3, 14-18. Newness of life, old man : Rm 6, 2-11 ; Col 3, 9-10.

Fundamentally we need to understand that the Old Man and New Man consist of essentially two different uses (and acts produced) by our faculties (eg. mind and will). The same faculties can collaborate or not with God's Grace. One way of acting if repeated will essentially produce, by the grace of God, a virtue, a good supernatural habit. This makes our "new man" grow. We can act in "neutral" ways, in the sense that our acts are not bad acts, but they are not activated by the Theological acts of Faith, Hope and Love. It is true that the main driving engine of spiritual growth includes these three acts. They allow the *New Man* in us to grow, to learn how God sees things (Faith), to see what goal we are pursuing (Hope) and how to act in general, that is, to see whether we love God and our brothers in Him. Any act, in fact, goes either in the direction of feeding the growth of the *New Man*, or the growth of the *Old Man*.

It is true that the soul itself is the mother of its spiritual life. We ourselves are the mother of our own new being. Self stays but it grows in depth and finds new roots.

As a consequence, however, the disappearance of the Old Creature is not the disappearance of ourselves!!

## God Loves Us <u>Always</u>

We often hear: "God loves us but not our sin", or, "God love the sinner but not his sin". Consider this, however: He loves our choices even the sinful ones for two reasons, not of course because of their sinfulness but because of on the one hand his respect for us, and on the other hand his capacity to offer us a further solution that will make us greater in his eyes.

In us we have "good" and "evil" as well as a "higher good". Our choice is always between good and evil. This is fine. But in case (God forbid) we choose evil, God is capable afterwards of helping us reach a higher good! It is as if evil has opened a new potential in us for something greater. In a way God can always have the "final word". But this depends on us. However, this never means that the door is open for sin! Knowing this and still sinning would be a real offence to his mercy and tempting Him: it is like throwing yourself from a high building and still expecting the angels to rescue you.

It is because of this understanding that not everything is lost after sin that we sing at Easter Vigil, while thinking of Adam's fault: "O happy fault that earned for us so great, so glorious a Redeemer."

In conclusion it would be fair to say that we can't mix the "old creature" and "the person". The "Old creature" is a way of acting, thinking seeing and is not the very self of this person, not the actual person itself.

When you take a shower after swimming in filthy water it is still you that emerges after the shower. This is a little like what occurs with the Old Man in us after purification. But it penetrates more deeply, in the sense that one has to introduce the notion of "purification" and "trans-formation" into the process.

Added to this, the act of sin adds new bad roots to the person, rooting the person in something else other than God. If your son or daughter does something bad do you love what they did? No. Do you love their act and the consequences of this act in them and outside of them? No. But you still love they themselves. The act of sin has just added a perished patch of cloth and bad roots to them, which only the experience of the Holy Spirit can show them from within, and which only He can remove; in fact we can refrain from sin, but the habits and bad roots which sin has created can only be removed by the Holy Spirit! Confession reconciles us with God, reopens the stream of the Grace of God, but it is the penance that we receive in confession that helps the Holy Spirit purify our being more deeply! This is why the penance has to be proportionate to the real gravity of the sin in order to help the grace of God enter deeply and change the person! The grace of confession is given but often not totally received and integrated. Therefore, the roots of our being can still hinder our future behaviour.

## Transformed in God

Do we know what it is to be transformed in God? It is advisable here to pause and consider what is needed for God to instruct us. Let us take the example of clay. We are created in God's Image and Likeness. The "image" of God that we are is the clay. The "likeness" is the form that the clay takes as a result of our acts. Because of sin, we lose only "the form". The "clay" is still there, but, is half-dead (see the parable of the Good Samaritan and the state in which the man was left on the side of the road).

Only the Holy Spirit can show us what is left after total purification.

## God's Bowels of Mercy

Let us enter into the bowels of God, the bowels of his being, of Him being Love. He loves us when we are sinners. Not for our sin, but for our sake. If we remove our sins, there stands our being, whole and entire. But be in no doubt: at any stage of our growth we are loved. Either at the beginning of the journey i.e. where the *Old Man* is in great evidence, or in the middle, or towards the end where the *New Man*pre dominates in the main.

Is God's love for us conditioned by His desire to have us Holy in front of Him? Would He continue to love us if we are sinning? Would He continue to love us even if we are far from Him and decided firmly to stay far away from Him? What is the "size" of his love for each one of us? Of course, He wants us to be with Him, but with our full collaboration. Does He know anything else other than "to love"? If we are far from Him, if his love can't reach us, He still loves us, waits for us. Of course, He cannot consent to any act we make that leads us further from Him. But despite our choice and our act, He continues to love us and considers that we need Him more than others need Him! However, He cannot and will never move our will or act for us. He cannot and will not ever impose his love on us!

He leaves us free if we want to abandon Him and go off! He will continue to love us and wait for us. But He will not force us. Never. His respect for our will and choices is absolute. This, ironically, even constitutes a handicap, a difficulty for Him! He can only send messages, warn, try to convince us, but He will never force us. This is our being made in his image! We were created as his partners, but He will not force us to be his!

On an even more positive note we can say that, our sins, and what they generate in us (the *Old Man*) are still, in a way, like a thin crust, ugly, but we are still there, underneath it. Like being in a prison, but it is still us! He loves us, He wants us free, out of this prison. Our sins are like an illness! Our illness cannot kill our soul! We are still there, loved as if we were without any illness.

I would say that a person who is far from God is, in a way, loved by God even more! Why? Because of his understanding of the person, his compassion. If we humans see a person in pain, thirsty, hungry, we feel compassion for this person! Why wouldn't God feel the same? But infinitely more!

It is true that we often hear this statement nowadays: "God loves us as we are". On the other hand, we hear also, the statement found above in the question: "he loves me as long as I am doing his will".

Both statements are correct. When He loves me, his gaze is capable of piercing the outer shell of my sin (the *Old Man*) to find me inside of this prison and darkness. Why would I deny

13

this? Why would this be underestimated? He loves me, here, despite my condition, despite my illness. He even loves me more.

Does He love my condition? My illness? My sin? We cannot ask or expect God to do so!

But paradoxically He has the utmost respect and understanding of my choices! First, because they come from me, who is created in his image! "Created in his image" is really a big mystery, because this enables me to stand in front of God and allows me to say to Him and his love: "yes" or "no"! What dignity we have been given! What power we have over God, over God's destiny!

We are as great as God, even if we are created by Him, in the sense that because of how we are created we have free will toward God himself...and He still loves us!

We can speak forever about the fact that God loves us, whichever the state in which we are in. Look at the behaviour of the father of the prodigal son. He still went to the top of the road of the road every day and waited for his son to return! Was he a happy person? No! Did he stay at home partying with this other son? No! He was "outside of himself", in pain, part of Him was missing from him. His son, "flesh of his flesh", "bone of his bones", had gone away... he couldn't force him to stay... but the father's state, God's state, is really bad! He is in huge pain! His son is away... "lost" ... It wasn't the Dad's choice! It was the son's choice! The father respected it! He waited... in pain, as if part of his body were missing, sad, sad, very sad. Crying! Waiting!

So yes, God loves us... we need to experience His love...

He is in a very bad state... He is out of himself... dead alive... part of Him is missing – his son – flesh of his flesh... He is in deep distress... He doesn't know what to do! He can't do that much! He respects his son's decision... He certainly sent messages... inquired... but He feels empty, infinitely sad..., He waits....

So, yes, God loves you... Jesus loves you....

We do not know what it means. It is unconditional though! Totally unconditional, because this is God's being and He cannot change his being!

# Where Is Your Heart?

First let me tell you a story. A man went to see a "sex worker" as some call them today. As it happened, he fell in love with her. Of course, she didn't. He kept going to see her, not for sex, but because he fell deeply in love with her. She failed to reciprocate this love. Finally, he shared what was happening to him with some of his male friends. Their explanation and advice were very plain and blunt: she is in it only for the money. He was hitting a dead end! No solution. His love for her wasn't reciprocated. It would not happen: no hope. It is true that, going on appearances, he was just seeing her for "sex", but he discovered progressively that in fact he wasn't really seeing her for physical gratification. He had a need to love; indeed, he had fallen in love.

You might be disgusted by the whole story. You might be harsh on him or her or on both. This is fine. It is your take on the story. The point I wish to make goes in a completely different direction. I find this story very revealing of something very deep about Christianity.

Don't we often read in the Old Testament (see below) about God talking to us through the Prophets, saying that each time we turn toward an idol and worship it, or become attached to it, this is the equivalent of spiritual adultery? Why so? Because God is the real Groom, our personal and unique Groom. This is why "worshiping" another god or idol is considered spiritual adultery. The following examples taken from the Old Testament will bear out the truth of this assertion:

"for like an *adulterous wife* this land is guilty of unfaithfulness to the LORD." (Hosea 1:2)

"You *prostituted* yourself with your lustful neighbours, the Egyptians, and increased your *promiscuity* to provoke Me to anger." (Ezekiel 16:26)

"Then you *prostituted* yourself with the Assyrians because you were not satisfied. Even after that, you were still not satisfied." (Ezekiel 16:28) (It is good to read the entire beautiful Chapter 16 in Ezekiel) "and they played in Egypt, *prostituting themselves* from their youth." (Ezekiel 23:3) "'you have *played the harlot with many lovers* — and you would return to Me?' declares the LORD." (Jeremiah 3:1)

Now here is how the story told above sheds an incredible light on our relationship with God. Let us try to understand in a little more depth what happened between the man and the woman. He ended up by needing her heart, and all that he was able to get was her body. She was perfectly capable of splitting love (matters of the heart) and physical demands. He wasn't. He needed her heart; she didn't involve her heart at all in the acts she was performing with him! He reached a point where he was going to see her again and again, not for the physical side of the relationship but for something deeper: he was hoping to touch her heart, while she on the other hand kept it away from him. She was happy merely to continue to offer her services.

This story could be a real story, but surprisingly it sheds an incredible albeit crude light on our relationship with God, with Jesus.

We could put blame on this lady from the start, because of her type of "work". We would be totally right in doing so. We could totally and radically condemn what she does. But, if we look at our relationship with God in greater depth, it will be easily found that in this story, the man who is in love with this woman is God, and it is we who are in her place. God wants to reach our heart and we are there "just for the money", that is, an exterior worship, just to get something out of it: either calm our conscience, or ask for some help from God. However, crucially, our heart remains elsewhere and we don't give it to God. We are unreachable! It is as if God is begging for our love, for our heart, and all that we can give Him is our body, our exterior worship, prayers, words, deeds. But our heart is kept well away, kept safe and inviolate.

This state of affairs could exist because of ignorance (we fail to realise that God needs our heart, a love that comes from the depths of our heart, the entire surrender of our being), or just because our heart is busy with other things, or persons.

In fact, we do not consider that God is the Groom. In both the Old Testament and the New Testament God presents himself as the true Groom. Jesus himself uses this expression various times! (see Matthew 9:15; 25:6; Luke 5:34) However, we tend to take it in a symbolic way, and it never crosses our minds that He has a Heart and that He is thirsty for us and that He needs some attention, love, some loving entrustment. It doesn't cross our minds that He has created us in His Image and His Likeness. We ourselves, by contrast, are not created in the image and likeness of our partners or future wife or husband. We are created *in His Image.* In this sense, when we find Adam searching for a helper who is like him, we can see in Adam (see Genesis 2) the New Adam, that is, Jesus, looking for this unique partner, that is, us – created *in His Image and Likeness* – or in other words *flesh of his flesh and bone of his bones*! Only God can fill a heart such as ours totally. Incredibly it is we who are called to fill God's heart with Joy, be His! What a Great Mystery!!

While Adam sleeps Eve is formed from one rib. Late 12th c.

We are, indeed, very good at fulfilling all our Christian duties ... the Commandments! Oh yes! We do. But, if we take a closer look, we are "in it for the money" – meaning our heart is not given to Jesus. We might have done everything we could, just as the woman above did – she offered all her services, perfectly – but our heart is not being given to Him, our loving attention, all our being is not being focused on Him and surrendered to Him.

The question we should ask ourselves here is: "Aren't we entering more deeply here into the first commandment, namely, 'You shall love God (your only Groom) with all your heart!'"? Are we in it with all our heart? Are we ready to surrender completely? Are we ready to discover the beauties of the Groom? Are we available to "fall in love" with Jesus?

And real love needs time! We can't say to a lover that we love him or her and not spend time with him/her! It doesn't make sense, because Loves finds its food in itself, in Love, in Loving, in exercising Love. Do we give Jesus this kind of attention? Do we spend time with Him without looking at our watch? Are we allowing ourselves to fall in love with Him?

Hmmm... these are the real questions that matter!

What have we done with our faith? Our understanding of our faith? Of the Gospel Teaching?

Aren't we sometimes "perfect" fulfillers of the commandments, like this woman, so perfect in the services she offers? But where is our heart?

It is so very easy to condemn people and their behaviour as "bad". However, sometimes aren't we in God's eyes a little bit like them?

It is worthwhile pondering on these words of the Evangelist: "For where your treasure is, there your heart will be also." (Matthew 6:21)

# God's Overwhelming Love For Us

Maybe you have come across this quotation from St. Therese of the Child Jesus:

*"Yes, I feel it; even though I had on my conscience all the sins that can be committed, I would go, my heart broken with sorrow, and throw myself into Jesus' arms, for I know how much He loves the prodigal child who returns to Him. It is not because God, in His anticipating Mercy, has preserved my soul from mortal sin that I go to Him with confidence and love..."* (St. Therese of the Child Jesus, Autobiographical Manuscripts, C, 36v°-37r°)

Many might say: well she is a saint; it is easier for her to say this. She was never in a state of grave sin. What does she know about being in state of sin, or even worse: to have on one's *"conscience all the sins that can be committed"*?! Since she herself never experienced grave sin, it is easier for her to say: *"I would go, my heart broken with sorrow, ..."*. She doesn't know what it is to feel the weight of sins, the feeling of guilt, the fear of God. The bottom line for these people is that they will hardly find it convincing and will continue to stand hard fast by their beliefs and attitudes.

Others might even say that God can get angry with us, seeing our sins. He can punish us severely for accumulated sins. The word "vengeance" will then be attributed easily to God.

We think – and we are right – that God finds our sins disgusting and repulsive. In addition, left to our natural thoughts and feelings that follow our sins, we are easily inclined to think that God wants to punish us for our deeds.

Of course, it goes without saying, that we are very far from St. Therese's understanding and perception of who God is. We don't instinctively go, "heartbroken with sorrow", to God. Some sort of residue of guilt or fear is still active in a recondite area of our conscience. After having committed sin, we don't bounce instinctively toward God, being sure that He will receive us with his arms wide open.

## Jesus' Revelation

The most refined and challenging point of the Lord's message to humanity – his Gospel – is the Revelation or the **true** face of God which it embodies. Jesus tells us that God is of immense bounty, deep goodness, unconditional love, infinite mercy, who constantly welcomes sinners. Compared to Moses' God, it must be said, there are some differences. So, in front of such a new revelation, one tends to doubt.

Indeed, this face of God was very new and challenging for his contemporaries, and is still very challenging for us, and will always continue to be challenging for future generations. People have shown great resistance to this Revelation. They have felt that Jesus was going against Moses, his Commandments and his punishments. They even challenged Jesus, and set traps for Him to prove Him wrong, to show that this image of God – the merciful God – He was presenting was just nonsense.

A well-known example of this series of traps set for Jesus concerns the Adulteress, in Chapter 8 in St. John's Gospel. Paradoxically, she is not the centre story. What is at the centre of these few verses (John 8:2-11) is not even Jesus himself, but the Revelation of the very nature of God He is unveiling before us. Not liking his new version of God, feeling that He was going

24

against Moses, they chose to challenge Him and see if He would be for Moses or against Moses so that they could accuse and rebuke Him, and finally declare that He was not a Prophet, not sent by God. Subsequently they found, very early one morning, a woman surprised in adultery, so that Jesus could not escape the case and had to decide if He was for Moses' God or against Him. Jesus, they thought, was cornered. They thought they finally had some proof against Him.

In fact, Moses had said that this woman, surprised very early in the morning in adultery, deserved to be stoned to death. Nobody could change Moses' Law and the Commandments! So, they cornered Jesus (as they thought) by putting his back to the wall. Would He, here also, say things that did not match what Moses had said and present a sweet and gentle image of God?

We know the outcome.

**Note:** some modern Exegetes consider that this passage of St. John is not by him, but rather by St. Luke. They totally disregard the fact that the dialectical movement between the Law of Moses and the Grace and Truth of Jesus permeates St. John's Gospel through and through. From the very first chapter, St. John announces one of the various themes of his Gospel: *"For the Law was given through Moses; Grace and Truth came through Jesus Christ."* (John 1:17)

We have St. Paul's words to add weight to those of St. John, when in Galatians 3:24 he shows that the Law is a pedagogue and exists to teach us what is right and what is wrong (Romans 3:21). He stresses that it does not save us, it cannot save us! Jesus came for sinners (Mt 9:13) says St. Matthew, to save them, to save what was lost (Mt 18:11).

25

In St. John the dialectic between the Law and Grace/Truth reaches its peak in Chapter 8, with the adulteress. It is at this point that St. John pulverises the debate and shows its emptiness and gives Jesus' Gospel a foretaste of victory over the limitations of Moses' Law.

Some people, admittedly, will still continue to have doubts regarding the deep and mind-blowing beauty of the face of God that Jesus is unveiling to us. Therefore, let us continue to explore the Gospel in order to find certainty, the certainty that this image of God that Jesus is showing us is really true, secure and eternal. It is the Gospel that unravels for us the very nature of God himself.

### Does God Retaliate or Punish?

In the Sermon on the Mount the Lord gives us his main charter, his core teaching. In Chapter 5 He uses a dialectical movement going from what Moses said to what He says. In this pendulum movement, the Holy Spirit through St. Matthew intends to show us that the Lord is the true Moses, the one Moses prophesised about in Dt 18: *"The LORD your **God will raise up for you a prophet** like me from among your brothers. You must listen to him. This is what you asked of the LORD your God at Horeb on the day of the assembly, when you said, "Let us not hear the voice of the LORD our God or see this great fire anymore, so that we will not die!" Then the LORD said to me, "They have spoken well. **I will raise up for them a prophet like you** from among their brothers. **I will put My words in his mouth**, and he will tell them everything I command him. And I will hold accountable anyone who does not listen to My words that that prophet speaks in My name."* (Dt 18:15-19)

Then, is Jesus' response in Matthew 5:38ss. He states Moses' Law first: *"You have learnt how it was said: Eye for eye and tooth for tooth."* Then immediately afterwards He reveals his Gospel to us, the Good news, the New Law:

*"But I say this to you: offer the wicked man no resistance. On the contrary, if anyone hits you on the right cheek, offer him the other as well; if a man takes you to law and would have your tunic, let him have your cloak as well. And if anyone orders you to go one mile, go two miles with him. Give to anyone who asks, and if anyone wants to borrow, do not turn away."* (Matthew 5:38-48)

We often read this teaching, being in awe, and forget to notice something very deep about it: in this text Jesus not only reveals to us the deeper aspects of his will, but He also reveals the true Face of God to us. How so? If God, who is God, is asking us, sinners, weak and limited as we are to act this way, to imitate Him (*"be sons of your Father in heaven"* (Mt 5), *"be perfect just as your heavenly Father is perfect"* (Mt 5)) this can only mean that God himself has been and still is the first one to act in this way and to be this way.

– Who is the wicked in the eyes of God? – The sinner! Sin is offending God; it is as if the sinner is hitting Him! – But how does God himself behave toward the sinner? ..."if anyone hits you on the right cheek, offer him the other as well" – *this* is His reply. This is how God acts toward us when we sin! We offend Him, we offend his holiness, but does He retaliate? No! He offers the other cheek! He can't ask us, sinners, limited and weak as we are, to behave in such a way, and not act Himself in the same way! God is Holy, Holy, Holy. Whenever we hurt Him, He is patient, He turns the other cheek; if we challenge Him to go with us for one mile or for a year, He goes with us

27

for two miles, or for two years. He gives us his patience, He gives us life (He doesn't kill us), He doesn't turn away! He stays there constantly waiting for us, patiently...

Paradoxically, these verses reveal more about God himself than anything else! This Charter is in fact a Revelation of God himself! God the Perfect, God the Holy, wants us to be like Him, to become his true sons and daughters, and He shows us how He behaves in the first place! This IS holiness! This IS his holiness.

### God Continues to Love us After We Sin

The Lord continues the revelation of the Father. He quotes Moses again by saying: "You have learnt how it was said: You must love your neighbour and hate your enemy."

And now He unveils the deep beauty of God's bounty: *"But I say this to you: love your enemies and pray for those who persecute you"* (Mt 5:). Who are God's enemies? The sinners! There is nothing, nothing in the world that makes us "enemies" of God other than sin! When we sin, we become God's enemies, we act in a threatening way, offending Him, wounding Him! How does He respond? Does He stop loving us because we do not deserve his love? Does He love only good people? Those who are in a state of Grace? Does He hate the rest of the world? Does He hate all those who are far from Him? No. God is Holy, and this holiness is unveiled by Jesus and we discover the mind-blowing Nature of God: God loves "us", and prays for "us", that is, He continues to send us his love and continues to knock at the door of our heart.

He simply cannot ask us, who are limited, to love our enemies and pray for them (which is by the way impossible for us to do without His Grace) and not apply it to Himself in the first place!

God loves his enemies (the sinners) ... constantly full of solicitude toward us, waiting for us, loving us, forgiving us, praying for us, hoping we will come back to Him, having his arms wide open all the time! He asks us to do that to our enemies, so wouldn't He be doing it all the time – He who is God, perfect and holy?

## What is God's Holiness?

We think that to say that God is holy means that He is very far from us, pure, elevated and sacred. We get scared by God's holiness, like Isaiah in Chapter 6:

*"In the year that King Uzziah died, I saw the Lord seated on a throne, high and exalted; and the train of His robe filled the temple. Above Him stood seraphim, each having six wings: With two wings they covered their faces, with two they covered their feet, and with two they were flying. And they were calling out to one another: "Holy, holy, holy is the LORD of Hosts; all the earth is full of His glory." At the sound of their voices the doorposts and thresholds shook, and the temple was filled with smoke. Then I said:* **"Woe is me, for I am ruined, because I am a man of unclean lips dwelling among a people of unclean lips; for my eyes have seen the King, the LORD of Hosts.**" (Isaiah 6:1-5)

True, when we get close to God's holiness, we feel how dirty we are, and we are filled with horror and shake out of fear.

Well the paradox here is that when Jesus presents God's Holiness He doesn't speak about a frightening being, a purity we imagine in our terms and that is beyond us. He, on the contrary, reveals to us what true purity is, true holiness: to love our enemy, to pray for him, to welcome him day and night, to keep our arms open for him! This is to be holy! This is to perform something super-human! Is this God fearsome? Isn't this God the gentle and humble of heart God?

God is good all the time! He is good toward us because He "is" Good, not because we deserve it. God loves because this is his nature! He doesn't change his nature! Jesus wants us to reach this level of divinisation, of transformation, of imitation of God. Jesus wants us to reach this level of holiness, of goodness, of bounteousness, of mercifulness... He wants us to become like God – the human bowels of God's Mercy.

*"in this way you will be sons of your Father in heaven, for he causes his sun to rise on bad men as well as good, and his rain to fall on honest and dishonest men alike. For if you love those who love you, what right have you to claim any credit? Even the tax collectors do as much, do they not? And if you save your greetings for your brothers, are you doing anything exceptional? Even the pagans do as much, do they not? You must therefore be perfect just as your heavenly Father is perfect.'"* (Mt 5)

This is a different image of God! This is, in a way, a different God.

Now, aren't we surer of what Therese said? If God wants us to forgive, to love our enemies, to pray for them, even if we had on our conscience all the sins that can be committed, they would not have any weight in front of God's Constant, Unfailing Love for each one of us. Who can fear God? Who can delay coming back to Him? Who can hesitate to go to Him? To draw closer to Him?

In the final analysis, then, which image of God are you following?

# Jesus' Embrace on the Cross

"Redemption", "Salvation", "Cross", "Crucified", are words/verbs we use so commonly. We understand them – certainly – but in a general way. We don't always get the chance to deepen them. Maybe because they are too obvious, too known, unquestionable.
Let us go deeper, if you will.

Good theology contemplates Jesus on the Cross, and the "work" He does in a deep way. The Cross (the Crucified, and His Work) has at least three layers:

1- the Suffering of **the Body** (tortured, beaten, bleeding…),

2- the Suffering of **the Soul** (carrying our darkness, our filth, our distance from God-Light (our sins), being torn between us and His own light, dislocated by that distance… the Lamb carrying our filth),

3- **the Spirit** (not the Holy Spirit but the eye of Jesus' Soul), in Peace and Joy, profoundly deep, not seen, not felt by his Body-Soul, but nonetheless present. He is realising the greatest thing on the Cross, the Will of the Father: coming out of himself, out of love, going toward us, grabbing us, and bringing us back to the Light, the Father's Home (see, below, the House on the right).

In a way, Jesus' arms are not held tight by the nails on the wood of the Cross. His Soul is holding us, very tight, his body holding our body, and his soul our soul. All this happens by the operation of the Holy Spirit (see, below, the dove on top of Jesus).

It is important to see deeper beyond appearances and reach the depth of the Love of God on the Cross and discover new depths in it.

This Cross (from El Salvador), depicts what I am trying to say about the deep reality happening on the Cross.

I hope that, by looking at this Cross, you'll be able to contemplate Jesus, the Good Shepherd, and what He did and is still doing for you. When St. Paul contemplated Jesus on the Cross, he said: "he loved me and died for me". Let us not live far from the surrounding area of the Cross, an area filled with the Love and Embrace of Jesus.

Here is what Jesus does when He sees us coming within the precincts of the Cross: "But while he was yet at a distance, his father saw him and had compassion, and ran and embraced him and kissed him." (Luke 15:20)

"What man of you, having a hundred sheep, if he has lost one of them, does not leave the ninety-nine in the wilderness, and go after the one which is lost, until he finds it? And when he has found it, he lays it on his shoulders, rejoicing." (Luke 15:4-5)

If you want to continue to contemplate this beautiful Cross, here are some suggestions:

Mary is the Flower below Jesus.

Another form of the same Cross has on the left, green fields, which represent Heavenly Grass (God's nature) for the Sheep. "Truly, truly, I say to you, [...] he who enters by the door is the shepherd of the sheep. To him the gatekeeper opens; the sheep hear his voice, and he calls his own sheep by name and leads them out. When he has brought out all his own, he goes before them, and the sheep follow him, for they know his voice. [...] Truly, truly, I say to you, I am the door of the sheep. [...] if anyone enters by me, he will be saved, and will go in and out and **find pasture**. [...] I came that they may have **Life**, and have it **abundantly**.

I am the good shepherd. The good shepherd lays down his life for the sheep. [...] I am the good shepherd; I know my own and my own know me, as the Father knows me and I know the Father; and I lay down my life for the sheep.

And I have other sheep, that are not of this fold; I must bring them also, and they will heed my voice. So, there shall be one flock, one shepherd. For this reason, the Father loves me, because I lay down my life, that I may take it again. No one takes it from me, but I lay it down of my own accord. I have power to lay it down, and I have power to take it again; this charge I have received from my Father." (John 10)

# God Wants to Love Us

– What is God's will? What is his deepest desire? What is He yearning for day and night?
– He just wants to love us!

What is it to love? It is to give everything and then to give oneself to the person one loves. So, if we say that God is love, that God wants to love us, we are saying: God wants to give Himself to us!

The big discovery that St. Therese makes toward the end of her life on the 9th June 1895, is that the torrents of God's love are actually compressed in Him because He simply cannot find anybody to receive them!

If you love somebody, it pleases you, I guess, to offer this person a present. And if you really love this person, and if you had enough means, you would like to buy this person the most beautiful and most valuable of presents there is. No? You would find great joy to give this present to the person you love, and you would be more than delighted to see his or her reaction.

Why would God be any different from you, in the sense that this is what He yearns for, this is his deepest desire, this is how He is?! This is his very nature. We do say that God's nature is love! But love is this constant outpouring of oneself. This **is** his nature.

One can gaze upon a powerful waterfall, say Niagara Falls, and see the sheer power of the water falling, its quantity, and its never-ending movement. Visualise it, or look at a picture, or even better watch a video of this outpouring of water. Then, after having been well impregnated buy this unique phenomenon, say: This IS God, this is how He is, what happens in Him! He can't change his being, his way of being and acting.

His deepest desire is to pour Himself out into us. Ironically, we are busy trying to understand his commandments, to find how to please Him that we forget the reality of this Being which we have in front of us, who He really is and what is happening in Him – He who has all this love compressed in his heart.

Every time we want to pray or think of God, we need first and foremost to gaze upon a powerful waterfall. Open our heart to Him and accept to receive his love humbly! It doesn't require a big effort to receive His Love, but it seems that on a practical level we still do struggle! We want to offer Him something, we want to make Him happy, we are searching for ways to put into practice his commandments, and we seem to go astray with the First Commandment: you shall love God with all your heart, energy, power. And what is it to love God if not to receive his love? This is the paradox: we think that we need to give, give, give, and we forget that we can't give what we don't have! To love God must first presuppose receiving his love in order to give it back to Him, enriched by our desire and choice to do so.

We often forget the invisible, or hidden verse that lies before the First Commandment: "I God, love you with all my heart, all my energy, all my power, all my being". This is in fact the hidden verse that lies before: "you shall love God with all your heart…". It is this hidden, almost shy, reality of God's love that is the foundation and basis of everything. With all his power, in an unconditional way, God wants to give himself to us.

**Note:** this verse is hidden. You won't find it explicitly said. But a proper and deep reading of the Scriptures, in the Holy Spirit, will open our eyes and show us this hidden reality: God confessing to each one of us in a clear irrevocable and unequivocal way that He loves us with all his being and power. Confessing love, such love, shows in fact that God is vulnerable. Hence the fact that the verse is hidden. It is up to us, with an Act of Faith in the Scripture as Word of God, to open our eyes to this amazing and mind-blowing reality: God says to you – to each one of us – personally, intimately, secretly, truly, uniquely, infinitely, eternally that He wants to give himself to you unconditionally, all the time.

St. John of the Cross endorses this when he says that contemplation consists in receiving! We can expand this even more to say: Prayer consists in receiving God's Love. Our

39

Christian Life, the meaning of our life here on earth is to accept to receive God's love.

It requires an effort. A delicate effort. It is easy and difficult to do at the same time. Easy because it is just about receiving. Difficult because this simple act, easy act, is not carried out by us! We are complicated beings, we are "multiple" (not unified, not yet one), we want to do other things, more palpable, more quantifiable, more rewarding for our spiritual ego, so we leave this effort at the bottom of our list and we rarely reach the bottom. God is left with this enormous, infinite thirst, and we are left there wandering, here and there, trying to be good Christians! Abandoning ourselves to who He is and to his outpouring seems very difficult! Incredibly this is so because it is unusual, because it looks such an insignificant thing! Surrendering to his being (not only to his will, but to his being, i.e. his outpouring of love) looks difficult. Accepting that this is what He wants, seems not to fit in with our understanding of Christianity. We have transformed Christianity into being good, acting good, doing good things. But we never question what it is to do a "good" thing? What is a good thing?
Why do we so easily forget the First Commandment? It is really the first, no other commandments come before it! We have morphed it into: be good and do good things! Or we have exchanged it for other commandments. Why do we forget God himself? We want to be sure (in our conscience) that we have offered or done some quantifiable good deeds; we want to reduce Christianity into something quantifiable, and we forget that after having accomplished all our "duties", we are still in debt to God for everything! You might fast, you might do amazing difficult or impossible deeds, you might kill yourself for God, but after all this, you can be sure that it is all nothing in the eyes of God. We easily exchange God for "religious" aspects of our Christian life, such as worship rites, or uses. We think then, in our conscience, that we are fine by doing this!
Poor us!

40

However, when we examine our conscience, who is the judge? A list of commandments or deeds? How then do we manage to escape from the First Commandment and its hidden verse? How then do we manage to escape from God's Love?

We are geniuses in inventing "ersatz" – replacement Commandments. We are very good at changing God's reality. Imagining God our way. In fact, is this the real God that we are facing? Or it is a nicely crafted, reduced and blurred image of Him that we have made? Who is God for me? This question should be there every day in our minds and in our daily quest! Who are you Lord? Reveal yourself to me as you are, I don't accept fake answers, but want the pure reality of your Being. I don't want to lean on my ill formed conscience, I want to be formed by your Holy Spirit, with every beat of my heart so I can really understand what you expect from me.

Conversion, daily conversion, is about this first! It is about accepting to let go of my certainties for better certainties given to me by the Holy Spirit, who shows me day after day the true image of God and not a nicely crafted but diminished one!

Our frequent prayer should say: teach me O Lord how to receive you. Teach me to accept a change in my understanding of you to a new understanding. Teach me to be very fervent, but fervent on the essential things, on who you are, what you really want to do in me… Teach me to receive your Love. Teach me the how to truly surrender to you. Teach me to accept my weakness and keep my gaze upon you and not on me! Teach me to accept my poverty, an ever more radical one, so that I can lean essentially on your Constant Outpouring of Love, of your Being in me. Teach me that the Love that comes from you is what you want me to give you, and nothing else.

41

To sum up then, the most concise expression of this prayer was given by St. Therese of the Child Jesus: "I always gave God only Love."

# The Revelation of God's Love

## The Parable of the Prodigal Son

In this article, we would like to discover some aspects of the Revelation of who God is, of the mind-blowing Love that the Lord is bestowing upon us.

Time and time again, the most crucial point in the Gospel, is the revelation of God's Face brought to us by Jesus: "No one has ever yet seen God. The only begotten God, the One being in the bosom of the Father, He has made Him known." (John 1:18) One of the most important aspects of the Lord's mission is to reveal for us the depths of God, to make Him known... to show us the true face of God. As we mentioned in another article, this new revelation of God wasn't readily welcomed by the Lord's contemporaries who questioned it loudly. Is this too good to be true? Too gentle to really function and manage us humans? Is it in contradiction with the God of Moses? The list is long.

One parable that is an outstanding example of the true face of God is the one known as "The Parable of the Prodigal Son." Here we have something really of another world, where Jesus introduces us to the depths of God's being. Let us first read the parable and call to mind all its parts.

## The Text of The Parable

*"11 And He said, "A certain man had two sons. 12 And the younger of them said to the father, 'Father, give to me the portion of the property falling to me.' And he divided the property between them. 13 And not many days later, the younger son having gathered together all, went away into a*

43

distant country, and there he wasted his estate, living prodigally.

14 But of him having spent all, there arose a severe famine throughout that country, and he began to be in need. 15 And having gone, he joined himself to one of the citizens of that country, and he sent him into his fields to feed pigs. 16 And he was longing to fill his belly from the pods that the pigs were eating, and no one was giving to him.

17 But having come to himself, he was saying, 'How many of my father's hired servants have abundance of bread, but here I am perishing with hunger? 18 Having risen up, I will go to my father, and I will say to him, "Father, I have sinned against heaven and before you; 19 no longer am I worthy to be called your son. Make me like one of your servants."'

20 And having risen up, he went to his father. And he still being far distant, his father saw him, and was moved with compassion, and having run, fell upon his neck and kissed him.

THE PRODIGAL SON

*21 And the son said to him, 'Father, I have sinned against heaven and before you; no longer am I worthy to be called your son.' 22 And the father said to his servants, Quickly bring out the best robe and clothe him, and give him a ring for his hand and sandals for his feet; 23 and having brought the fattened calf, kill it, and having eaten, let us be merry. 24 For this son of mine was dead and is alive again; he was lost and is found.' And they began to be merry.*
*25 And his elder son was in the field, and while coming up, he drew near to the house; he heard music and dancing. 26 And having called near one of the servants, he began inquiring what these things might be. 27 And he said to him, 'Your brother is come, and your father has killed the fattened calf, because he has received him in good health.' 28 But he was angry, and was not willing to go in. And his father, having gone, was begging him. 29 And answering, he said to his father, 'Behold, so many years I serve you, and never did I disobey a commandment of yours; and never did you give to me a young goat, that I might make merry with my friends. 30 But when this son of yours came, the one having devoured your living with prostitutes, you have killed the fattened calf for him!' 31 And he said to him, 'Son, you are always with me, and all that is mine is yours. 32 But it was fitting to make merry and to rejoice, because this brother of yours was dead and is alive again; and he was lost and is found.'"* (Luke 15:25-32)

## Discovering God

This parable was originally offered by the Lord to the Pharisees and the Doctors of the Law of Moses. This is how the parables of Chapter 15 are presented: *"Now all the tax collectors and the sinners were drawing near to Him to hear Him. 2 And both the **Pharisees** and the **scribes** were grumbling saying, "This man receives sinners and eats with them.""* (Luke 15:1-2) The main thrust of the parable seems to be aimed at the scribes and the Pharisees, so that modern exegesis considers that the parable should be named: "The Parable of The Elder Son". The reason for this is that his behaviour depicts that of the Pharisees and the Scribes for whom sinners were irreconcilably damned and who felt that treating sinners this way was in keeping with the Law of Moses. Therefore, the were shocked to see that the Lord received sinners and drew closer to them (see verse 22 onward). The Pharisees preferred to condemn the sinners and to exclude them. In fact, the word "Pharisee" itself means "the chosen", "the selected", "the pure".

The scribes and doctors of the Law were highly conversant with Moses' Law and how it was capable of being very harsh on sinners. A prodigal son, for instance, should normally be treated the following way according to the Moses' Law:

*"If a man has a stubborn and rebellious son who does not obey his father and mother and does not listen to them when disciplined, 19 his father and mother are to lay hold of him and bring him to the elders of his city, to the gate of his hometown, 20 and say to the elders, "This son of ours is stubborn and rebellious; he does not obey us. He is a glutton and a drunkard." 21 Then all the men of his city will stone him to death. You must purge the evil from among you, and all Israel will hear and be afraid."* (Dt 21,18-21)

To stone to death is something very harsh and radical to enforce the heinous nature of sin, yet Jesus not only fails to condemn the sinners, but He also draws closer to them, sits with them, eats with them. Jesus' behaviour strongly clashes with Moses' Law. It is to help the Pharisees and the Doctors of the Law to get to gain new understanding that this parable is given. The Lord would like to help them soften their hearts and welcome their repentant brothers.

Indirectly, then, through the immensely kind-hearted Father, we are meant to learn how God sees sinners. The Father in the parable, indeed, represents God the Father. Through the parable, Jesus is offering us a very human heart, the broken heart of this father who saw his son asking for his part of the inheritance, and deciding to leave his home and go and spend his money with prostitutes. Jesus does this in order to explain to us just who God **IS** and how He reacts and feels toward sinners. The newness of this method (although used in the Old Testament: « "Can a mother forget the baby at her breast and have no compassion on the child she has borne? Though she may forget, I will not forget you! » (Isaiah 49:15)) really staggers belief because it shows us that God is more human than we are, more tender and caring of us. In trying to know God, we compare Him to ourselves – like human beings. This method used in this parable and elsewhere means that being God doesn't deprive Him of our human qualities but instead, it multiplies them or intensifies them infinitely. Hence, if we are good, God's bounty is infinitely greater. But "being good" is a quality that we humans can know, understand. The fact that God is God doesn't make Him alien to our human qualities or virtues, it just intensifies them, put them to the infinite degree.

The Lord himself indicated this path or method in other places in the Gospel when He said : « *Therefore, if you, being evil, know how to give good gifts to your children, **how much more** will your Father in the heavens give good things to those asking Him!* » (Matthew 7:11). The phrase « how much more » is an indication to us of a method of knowing God. Bottom line: God is infinitely much more human than we are. What a paradox! What a discovery!

Let us always remember this method of reading the Scripture in order to know God. We are created "in the image and likeness" of God. His "likeness" in us is diminished because of our sins.

Therefore, his infinite tenderness is much reduced in us, but in order to know God, we can still use whatever tenderness we find in our human life and extrapolate from it!

Before stopping at a key verse, let us just remember the Father's behaviour toward his youngest son at the start of the parable. When the son asked him for his part of the inheritance, the Father, gave him his part. He didn't deny him his freedom, his energy, his desires, his goals. In the case of each and every one of us God leaves us free throughout our lives.
Let us now stop at verse 20 and ponder on it.

### God's Visceral Love for Each One of Us

Sometimes we think that God's love for us is just a decision He makes, but we don't necessarily see the link between God himself, his being on one hand and his love for us on the other. We fail to see the hidden link between us and Him, the link that makes Him feel the void of our absence, that pains Him physically to the core for our absence and loss. It gives God feelings. It shows that God can suffer because of us. How can we ever express this…? The cold uniform equanimous image of God the philosophers show us seems here to fade and be replaced by a much more human God, a God that we can understand, and feel for. This is simply mind-blowing.

Let us see what the text says about the Father:

*"And having risen up, he went to his father. And he still being far distant, his father saw him, and was moved with compassion, and having run, fell upon his neck and kissed him."* (Luke 15:20)

The phrase "being far distant" in the line: "And he still being far distant, his father saw him" means that the Father used to go to the main road and look out for his son. He was sad, he had lost his own child. He didn't give up hope, however, but stayed there waiting for his son. Then one day he saw him. He was able not only to see him but to notice his state, his clothes, the fact that he had lost weight and wasn't clean. But this was still his son and he was deeply "moved with compassion." Here, indubitably, we witness a God not insensitive to our state. He suffers. He is sad because of our state.

Let us pause for a moment to note that, in Greek the expression is "splagchnizomai" which means "to be moved in the inward parts", i.e. "to feel compassion". "splagxnízomai", from "splanxna", 'the inward parts,' especially the nobler entrails – the heart, lungs, liver, and kidneys. These parts gradually came to denote the seat of the affections" (WS, 111).)

Did he wait for his son to arrive? Did he prepare himself to level harsh criticism at him and reproach him for his behaviour? Was he angry at him? No. Quite the opposite: "he ran toward him," he wanted to meet him, to touch him to hug him to get him close to his heart. He didn't wait. He couldn't wait! Do we understand God's Heart? God's viscera? Did he go slowly? He ran! Ran!
You would expect him to say angry or highly critical words to his son! To rebuke him! None of this happened! He "fell upon his neck" …. The Father threw himself upon the neck of his son! Aren't we God's children? Created in his image and likeness? It comes as no surprise, then, that He fell upon his neck, he embraced him, he hugged him!

As if this were not enough there is more… He kissed him profusely. Translators try to render the Greek word in some of the following possible translations of what the Father did: kissed him "repeatedly", "profusely", "fervently", "affectionately", "passionately", "like a torrent of kisses".

49

This is the reaction of God himself! This is what He does to the sinner! He needed to feel that close to his son! He hugged him and kissed him profusely. Remember, his son is dirty! God didn't feel any disgust toward the state of his son! He didn't say to him: go, have a good bath, and put on new clothes and then we need to talk. None of this! None of this! He hugged him at length… he kissed him! To the one who had betrayed him and his trust, to the one who had lost all his hard-earned money on prostitutes, God gives back a kiss! A long hug and plenty of kisses!

## Who can understand?

Not only that, but God goes on to defend the younger son when talking to the elder one who didn't agree with this behaviour! He took time to explain to the elder son that his younger son had been lost, and that he was finally back and that they needed to celebrate!

Who can understand this? Who can fathom "who God is"?

He didn't blame his wasteful son once for what he had done! He wanted to celebrate. He offered him new clothes, a ring, and a big celebration. This is God!

Of course, it is difficult for the average human being to accept this image of God! One feels some justice should be implemented here! No, none! One feels some fairness should be applied! No!! Not our fairness, but another more comprehensive one!

As above-mentioned, we have the impression that the father used to go out of his house every day, to go and gaze, check on the horizon to see if his son was returning. He knew very well that far from the paternal house only harm could happen to him! He knew, because it is easy to guess, the state in which his son was when he had made the demand of his father and left. He is worried, he feels

50

anguish, he is only half-alive because his love and compassion for his son make him one with his son with all his heart, all his soul, so that he can feel all that his son feels.

It comes as no surprise then that the way the father receives his son is unconditional and full of love and tenderness. This **is** God! He didn't ask him to give an account of all that he had done; he didn't judge him as the elder son would do! The latter, indeed, with his vision of justice doesn't correspond to the true Face of God. It is imperative, therefore, that we drop the elder son's understanding of justice and clothe ourselves with the sentiments of God!

To reiterate once again: the father jumps on his son's neck and kisses him tenderly and profusely! This passage reveals to us God's Face! This passage is deeply moving! God waits for the human being, God waits for the human being to turn towards Him, to receive his love, his tenderness.

Another passage from the Gospel where God's tenderness shows is the following: *"Jerusalem, Jerusalem, killing the prophets, and stoning those having been sent to her, how often I have wanted to gather your children, the way that a hen gathers her brood under the wings, and you were not willing."* (Luke 13:34) This passage moved St. Therese of the Child Jesus, so that when in the garden of her monastery she saw some chicks she remembered this passage and cried for joy contemplating God's tenderness:

*"Descending the steps leading into the garden, she saw a little white hen under a tree, protecting her little chicks under her wings; some were peeping out from under. Thérèse stopped, looking at them thoughtfully; after a while, I made a sign that we should go inside. I noticed her eyes were filled with tears, and I said: "You're crying!" She put her hand over her eyes and cried even more. "I can't explain it just now; I'm too deeply*

51

*touched." That evening, in her cell, she told me the following, and there was a heavenly expression on her face: "I cried when I thought how God used this image in order to teach us His tenderness towards us. All through my life, this is what He has done for me! He has hidden me totally under His wings! Earlier in the day, when I was leaving you, I was crying when going upstairs; I was unable to control myself any longer, and I hastened to our cell. My heart was overflowing with love and gratitude."* (Yellow notebook, 7 June n°1)

Again, this tenderness and love is reflected in the father's reaction when his son says: *"Father, I have sinned against heaven and before you; no longer am I worthy to be called your son."* But the father says to his servants: "22 *'Quickly bring out the best robe and clothe him, and give him a ring for his hand and sandals for his feet; 23 and having brought the fattened calf, kill it, and having eaten, let us be merry. 24 For this son of mine was dead and is alive again; he was lost and is found.'"* Let us note that the father doesn't make any reproach to his son! He immediately receives him without any conditions. The father is happy to have his son back. He could have made him feel guilty. Not at all. On the contrary he explains why he is happy: *"this son of mine was dead and is alive again; he was lost and is found."*
Indeed, we are being confronted by a mind-blowing revelation of who God **is**! Of his being, of his feelings, of his behaviour, his love! Yes, the Son of God, the Lord Jesus, came to reveal to us the true God. Who could have imagined God like this? God the Father wants to hug you, at length and tenderly! He doesn't want you to go. He wants you to stay with Him! He is very happy to have you! He rejoices and find his delight in you! Take heart – you are truly loved and wanted!

# The Hidden Verses

**Summary:** this chapter intends to deepen our understanding of God's Commandments as summarised by Jesus. In doing so, we will discover the existence of two very important though hidden verses.

## Introduction

*"Truly you are a God who hides himself, O God of Israel, the Saviour."* (Is 45:15) These words of Isaiah tell us that God is… in a constant hidden position. In which sense can we say that God is "hidden" and that what we know of Him is very little considering who He is?

What is it exactly that we know about God? We presume that we possess a good deal of knowledge about Him. However, in doing so, unconsciously, we are constantly making judgements about God! Who He is; How He sees things; How He sees us, judge us, judges others, facts, deeds and situations. We think we know. The Scriptures reveal God to us, but at the same time, they keep a great deal of Him hidden.

Our job is to dig deep! Will it not be our "mission" for all eternity, to delve always deeper into God, discovering at every heartbeat of eternity, a new aspect in God, leaving us in great awe?

By contrast and mistakenly, we tend to limit God with the workings of our brain. But God is limitless, infinite, uncreated. In a way He certainly is the main object of our exploration and research. Why, then, at a certain point in our Christian life, do we reach a point of "satisfaction" thinking that our thirst for knowing God has been quenched and we stop wanting to know more? And when we say "to know" we need to intend it in the deep Biblical meaning, used to denote the human relationship between a man and a woman.

God, however, reveals himself to us, in Jesus and through Jesus' Words and deeds. God continues in time, after Jesus' Resurrection, through forty days and Ascension, to lead us to the fullness of Truth with the coming of the Holy Spirit. This embodies in great part the meaning of our life. This prepares us for Eternity, which will be, in fact, the continuation of this divine exploration of God. Otherwise, if we consider it, if this wasn't the meaning of our life and the contents of Eternity, the latter would be extremely boring. Imagine sitting for the rest of your Eternity in front of a screen- saver picture of God. Killingly boring. So, let us get ready for our Eternal job and start exploring God himself, wanting to know Him (biblical knowledge not mind and reason knowledge), which means experiencing Him, receiving Him and receiving the Revelation He makes of himself to us.

Let us always assume that we are rather on the blind side, and that we need to see Him! We need to discover new aspects of Him! This is why human life on earth cannot be boring! It is a constant exploration, making relentless discoveries of God himself. God exists! He deserves to be known and loved for himself alone. We dedicate teams of people and money for research in technology, matter, the universe, atoms, medicine.... Do we do the same for God?

Aside from this being the task of every Christian, being a monk, by comparison, should particularly have as an object this research. Not a purely intellectual research. Not an accumulation of PhDs... though there is nothing wrong with this, but this type of research is something altogether different. Even the PhDs in Theology should be on a personal quest. Being a Theologian should be like being a monk twice over, in the sense that the vocation for searching for who God is finding Him, having the experience of Him, and should be the essence of the mission of the Theologian. Otherwise, it would be better to remove the prefix "Theos" from Theo-logian.

The Scriptures offer us an amazing opportunity to delve deeper into God. They are not sleek, streamlined or plain! They are full of mysteries, unexpected things, obstructions, "irregularities", difficulties, obstacles... This is done on purpose, with the intention of God hiding himself under a rough shell, almost dissuading us from looking into it and through it. Only the persistent believer, the resilient one, would undertake to dig!

Look at the archaeologist. Look at the Geologist, Palaeontologist, Geoarchaeologist. They search, unearth, try to understand and read history through remains, through rocks. Even the Astrophysicist undertakes similar research but in the cosmos.

Is digging about pure exegesis of the text? Is it only about grinding up the text? Isn't it also about something slightly different? Indeed it is, for the text of the Old and of the New Testament contain much more than the literal explicit meaning we find in it. The literal meaning is a very minute (important though it is and unmissable) morsel, hiding a huge being: God himself.

Questioning the text, challenging our understanding of the text is needed in order to go off the beaten track and keep alive in us this sense of awe when face to face with the infinite God.

We know how challenging and tough the Old Testament (and also many passages of the New Testament) can be. It has also some of the most beautiful and unsurpassed passages about God. A great Paradox.

Let us look at one of the most commonly known passages of the Bible and see how many surprises it is concealing for us. It is the passage where Jesus summarises Moses' Commandments.

The act of summarising is a very important act because usually the risk one incurs in doing so is to diminish the content, reduce it, take away important parts of it. Jesus dares go for the challenge of summarising the entire commandments and He does it in a very specific way. He gives us a "portable" "easy" summarised way to remember the summary of all our duties. But what is there that is more than what the eye can see?

There are three plus one different accounts about the summarising of the Commandments. Three are found in the so-called "synoptic Gospels" i.e. Matthew, Mark and Luke. There Jesus offers two commandments. And we have an apparently completely different form in the Gospel of St. John where Jesus offers us one summarising commandment that He calls: the new commandment (John 13:31-35). John will later say in his first letter that it is not "new" as such (see 1 John 2:7-8), but new in Jesus and in us.

Let us first consider and read the three synoptic two-commandments versions.

## Matthew: 22: 34-40

"34 And the **Pharisees**, having heard that He had silenced the Sadducees, were gathered together the same day. 35 And one of them, a lawyer (an expert in the Jewish Law), questioned Him, **testing** Him, 36 "Teacher, which commandment is **the greatest** in the Law?" 37 And He said to him, ""You shall love the Lord your God with all your heart, and with all your soul, and with all your mind." (Dt 6:1-19) 38 This is the great and first commandment. 39 And the second is like it: 'You shall love your neighbour as yourself." (Lev 19:18) 40 On these two commandments hang all the Law and the Prophets."" (Mt 22:34-40)

## Mark: 12: 28-34

"28 And one of the scribes having come up, having heard them reasoning together, having seen that He answered them well, questioned Him, "Which commandment is **the first** of all?"
29 Jesus answered, "The foremost is, 'Hear this O Israel: The Lord our God is One Lord, 30 and you shall love the Lord your God with all your heart, and with all your soul, and with all your mind, and with all your strength.' 31 The second is this: 'You shall love your neighbour as yourself.' There is not another commandment greater than these." 32 And the scribe said to Him, "Right, Teacher. You have spoken according to truth that He is One, and there is not another besides Him, 33 and to love Him with all the heart and with all the understanding and with all the strength, and to love the neighbour as oneself is **more important than all the burnt offerings and sacrifices**." 34 And Jesus, having seen him that he answered wisely, said to him, "You are not far from the kingdom of God." And no one dared to question Him any longer." (Mk 12:28-34)

## Luke: 10: 25-28

"25 One day an expert in the law stood up to test Him. "Teacher," he asked, "what must I do to **inherit eternal life**?" 26 "**What** is written in the Law?" Jesus replied. "**How do you read it**?" 27 He [the expert in the law] answered, " 'Love the Lord your God with all your heart and with all your soul and with all your strength and with all your mind' and 'Love your neighbour as yourself.' " 28"You have answered **correctly**," Jesus said. "**Do this** and you will live." 29 But wanting to justify himself, he asked Jesus, "And who is my neighbour?" (Luke 10:25-28)

(Then in order to explain who "my neighbour" is Jesus tells us the parable of the Good Samaritan where not a new type of neighbour is offered but another type of Jew is offered: a Samaritan who acts better than a Jew.)

Let us also remember the texts of the Old Testament Jesus is quoting:

## Deuteronomy: 6: 1-19

"1 These are the commands, decrees and laws the Lord your God directed me to teach you to observe in the land that you are crossing the Jordan to possess, 2 so that you, your children and their children after them may fear the Lord your God as long as you live by keeping all his decrees and commands that I give you, and so that you may enjoy long life. 3 Hear, Israel, and be careful to obey so that it may go well with you and that you may increase greatly in a land flowing with milk and honey, just as the Lord, the God of your ancestors, promised you. 4 Hear, O Israel: The Lord our God, the Lord is one. 5 **Love the Lord your God with all your heart and with all your soul and with all your strength.** 6 These commandments that I give you today are to be on your hearts. 7 Impress them on your children. Talk about them when you sit at home and when you walk along the road, when you lie down and when you get up. 8 Tie them as symbols on your hands and bind them on your foreheads. 9 Write them on the doorframes of your houses and on your gates.

10 When the Lord your God brings you into the land he swore to your fathers, to Abraham, Isaac and Jacob, to give you—a land with large, flourishing cities you did not build, 11 houses filled with all kinds of good things you did not provide, wells you did not dig, and vineyards and olive groves you did not plant — then when you eat and are satisfied, 12 be careful that you do **not forget the Lord**, who brought you out of Egypt, out of the land of slavery. 13 **Fear the Lord** your God, **serve him only** and take your oaths in his name. 14 **Do not follow other gods**, the gods of the peoples around you; 15 for the Lord your God, who is among you, **is a jealous God** and his **anger will burn against you**, and **he will destroy you** from the face of the land. 16 **Do not put the Lord your God to the test** as you did at Massah. 17 **Be sure to keep the commands** of the Lord your God and the stipulations and decrees he has given you. 18 Do what is right and good in the Lord's sight, **so that it may go well with you** and you may go in and take over the good land the Lord promised on oath to your ancestors, 19 thrusting out all your enemies before you, as the Lord said." (Dt 6:1-19)

## Leviticus 19:18:

"Do not seek revenge or bear a grudge against any of your people, but love your neighbour as yourself. I am the LORD."
Let us now focus on Matthew's version.

## The Two Commandments

*"34 And the **Pharisees**, having heard that He had silenced the Sadducees, were gathered together the same. 35 And one of them, a lawyer (an expert in the Jewish Law), questioned Him, **testing** Him, 36 "Teacher, which commandment is **the***

*greatest in the Law?" 37 And He said to him, "'You shall love the Lord your God with all your heart, and with all your soul, and with all your mind.' [Dt 6:1-19] 38 This is the great and first commandment. 39 And the second is like it: 'You shall love your neighbour as yourself.' [Lev 19:18] 40 On these two commandments hang all the Law and the Prophets.'"* (Mt 22:34-37)

Before entering deeper into the Commandments as Jesus summarises them, let us consider a few initial points. First of all it is a Pharisee who is talking to Jesus. But who are the Pharisees? They comprise a group of people who consider themselves as the elect, the chosen, the elite-group of God, the pure. All their efforts are concentrated on offering a pure practice of God's Law, the Torah. Thus, when a Pharisee challenges Jesus, what is at stake is Jesus' orthodoxy, the purity of Jesus' faithfulness to Moses. In the text, it is not only a Pharisee, but a Doctor of the Law, an expert in the Torah who ventures to challenge Jesus' orthodoxy. Why is this so? The answer is that Jesus' Message, the Good News, seems to many too "new", too different, from Moses' Law. Jesus doesn't speak too much about very detailed laws and rules, He doesn't speak too much about exterior practices of the Law, therefore by default He seems to be dismissing it. By contrast, however, Pharisees look at sacrifices, other added laws, a literal reading of the law and rules. The temptation then is to embody all our duties toward God into a list of commandments and rules that end up giving us the illusion that we are really pleasing God. Another important reason why Jesus' Teaching appears "new" is because instead of focusing on a minute and detailed way of practising the hundreds of Jewish traditional commandments, Jesus focuses on exercising Mercy toward our brothers and sisters. This seems to turn the Law upside down where the Law appears to be a focus of our duties towards God himself and worship.

**Note: The Newness of Jesus' Teaching.** If one considers the different versions of the two commandments in the New Testament, one easily notices a movement in this direction, i.e. toward the love of our neighbour! At first sight it could be misunderstood, as is happening with the Pharisees, and one could think that Jesus seems to be changing Moses' Law and horizontalizing it. However, this is not the case at all.

In Matthew and Mark, we are still dealing with a summary. (Please see above texts) With Luke we already start the shift: "Who is my neighbour?" says the Pharisee and gives Jesus the opportunity to offer us the amazingly disturbing parable of the Good Samaritan. He flips the question: instead of telling us who our neighbour is, Jesus tells us that a non-Jew (or a non-Christian) can be better than they, the guardians of the Law, in loving our neighbour! Instead of telling the Pharisee about the object of love, i.e. on which category of people he should focus and adding the Samaritan, He flips attention to the Pharisee himself, i.e. the subject of love, the one who loves.

(Samaritans, compared to the Jews, were true heretics. Imagine who could be our Samaritan today! I leave it up to you.)

Finally, with St. John, instead of having two commandments, Jesus unites them in his person, giving himself as the perfect living implementation of the Law: "love one another as I have loved you". He even calls it "my commandment"! Acting as God! God only gives commandments! Jesus acts here as a legislator. Plus, He seems here to be turning Moses' Law upside down, by placing the love of our neighbour as a priority. In fact, however, it is an optical illusion! The small expression "as I loved you" changes the commission entirely.

As we can see, in summarising Moses' Law in the four Gospels, we find that there is a true progression:

61

1- Matthew-Mark, 2- Luke, 3- John. In this, Jesus' teaching appears "new" to his contemporaries.

The truth is that Jesus has perfected Moses' Law. He didn't come to abolish it but rather to add a new depth to it. Jesus says: you have been told: do not kill. I say to you: do not hate your enemy – on the contrary, love your enemy and pray for him! Jesus delves deep; He can purify our heart, transform it with his Holy Spirit, and allow it to do something normally impossible: to love our enemy. In this also Jesus' teaching appears "new".

This is why the text adds: "questioned him, testing him". Jesus claims to be not only a prophet but The Prophet mentioned by Moses' prophecy (Deuteronomy 18), the Messiah himself. So, the Pharisees, challenged by his new teaching want to see who He is, and test his orthodoxy, see if He is abiding by the Truth as they know it from Moses.

In the midst of the thick forest of the commandments and rules, the Pharisees want to see how Jesus understands and summarises the Law, the Torah. This is part of the challenge. They test his understanding of the Law. It is not only a copy-paste answer, but by summarising one also interprets. They, in fact, are challenging Jesus to make sense of the Law, to see how He understands it – to show them his knowledge of the Law.. Show us your knowledge. Jesus accepts the challenge and in his answer He will in fact challenge all of us (the Pharisees and we Christians, readers of the Gospel). Jesus will bring together two texts, one from Deuteronomy and one from Leviticus. One talks about our duties toward God and one about our duties toward our neighbour. One can say that it is a way, first, of going back to the ten commandments of the Law and secondly of summarising the ten commandments, classifying them into two categories, the first ones that focus on God and the second ones that focus on our neighbour. (The numbering of the commandments is "3 and 7" or "4 and 6" depends on the versions or traditions. See this article) His choice seems to satisfy the Doctor of the Law and the Pharisees. Matthew doesn't mention this aspect but Mark, in his longer version says: *"And no one dared to question Him any longer."* (Mk 12:34)

Let us also not forget the authoritative and powerful conclusion of Jesus in Matthew: *"On these two commandments hang all the Law and the Prophets."'"* (Mt 22:40) Jesus, thereby, is saying that if truly fulfilled, these two commandments not only summarise but also overshadow the entire Law and the Prophets, in the sense that all other commandments proceed from them. If I fulfil these two, all the others will be fulfilled because they depend on them like the "body" depends on the "head".
Here seems to end the story, in Matthew's account.

## The First Hidden Verse

Instead of continuing our journey through the three other versions (Mark, Luke, John) I would like to stop and ponder on the two Commandments, as summarised by Jesus in Matthew.

Jesus here, when quoting Moses, seems to be giving once again the Law, in a summarised way. He is asking us Christians to focus on these two commandments. He clearly says that they really and truly summarise Moses' Law. This act of summarising is part of Jesus' teaching. Let us look at it then as coming from Jesus, as a doctoral act on his part.

God, in Jesus and through Jesus, gives us his Commandments:
*"37 'You shall love the Lord your God with all your heart, and with all your soul, and with all your mind.' (Dt 6:1-19) 38 This is the great and first commandment. 39 And the second is like it: 'You shall love your neighbour as yourself.'"* (Mt 21:37-39)

63

Let us start by speaking boldly and humanly, just for the sake of getting a truer understanding and not in any way lacking respect toward God and his Sanctity. The start of Jesus' statement is bold and lacks gentleness. Without any preamble, God says this is what I want you to do: 'You shall love the Lord your God with all your heart, and with all your soul, and with all your mind.' He wants "all" my heart, "all" my soul, "all" my mind, my energy, my being! This is ferocious as a demand! Imagine a young man talking to his date saying: you must love me with all your heart, all your soul, all your mind, all your energy. What would be her response? To flee! This is an unbearable way of treating a young lady! Who is he to ask for such a thing: all... all... all.... There would be nothing left in us after that if all our being were involved in loving God! Yet we *are* called to be totally devoured by God! Indeed, He says that He is a devouring fire (*Deuteronomy* 4:24 and *Hebrews* 12:29).

God here looks like a wild tyrant without any mercy, wanting all of our being. And "out of love"! Again, let me repeat that I have no intention of offending God's Holiness, I am just trying to address in human terms the commandment as it is without diminishing it, because we very rarely consider how bold and roughshod it is! God is asking us – out of love – to give Him everything! What is left in us? Do we realise that this is our religion? Do we realise that this is our faith? Do we realise how absolute is the first commandment – that He wants all of our being? Do we realise how abrupt and almost violent and unbearable is the demand! In fact, it can be questioned now, that since nothing is left of us, is there any room for another commandment?

It is important to meditate and ponder on the radicalness of God's first and most important commandment: He wants all of our being for Him! Out of love! It is a sudden and frightening request.

To love is to give everything and give oneself. To give oneself! So, if God is asking me to love Him with all my heart, all my soul, my strength and thoughts, He is in fact asking me to give Him all my being: heart, soul, energy... Just think...He approaches us and the first thing He requests from us is all of ourselves! Nothing less than everything. A sudden and shocking way to approach us. He truly is the creator of his people He is talking to in Deuteronomy and He is their saviour: He saved them from Egypt and freed them. But still... the demand on Mount Sinai is quite abrupt.

Why isn't the introduction to this verse smoother, gentler? I am deeply convinced that this verse in Deuteronomy where God states his first commandment, is preceded by a hidden verse that introduces it. This hidden verse goes something like this: "I am YHWH your God. I do love you with all my heart, all my mind, all my strength... and therefore I can ask you in return to love me in the same way." This verse is hidden. It is like God's secret, God's vulnerable area. God's powerful feelings toward each one of us.

This verse is the truth! Nobody can challenge this statement unless we deviate from orthodoxy. God really loves us, is at the door of our heart, waiting, wanting to give himself to us entirely, not wanting to keep anything to himself. This is his truth, his deep truth, a discreet but true confession!

Comparing the contemplating of the manifestation of God's Love (Jesus on the Cross), St. Paul says: "he loved me and died for me", while St. John says: "that much God loved the world that He gave his only son his beloved." Significantly, the Greek text puts "that much" at the beginning of the sentence, which is grammatically correct in Greek, but it goes to underline the power of the statement and its intention).

65

Taking all this into consideration we now can see the right order in a fuller light as follows:

1- I am God, your God, and I do love you with all my heart, strength, mind… (hidden verse)

2- Therefore, I invite you to respond to my love, giving me the same: i.e. everything.

**Note:** first and foremost, God loves us not because we are good, or we deserve it or merit his love. It would be an error to think that! He loves us because this is his very nature, because He is Good, Goodness itself! He can't change his nature! The only thing He knows and does is to love, i.e. to give himself. He is like an almighty waterfall, that can't stop itself from falling, from giving himself, from coming out of himself.

But still, because we are made in his image and likeness there is a mysterious attraction that He feels toward us. We are capable of receiving his love, and He is divinely thirsty to give himself! Jesus once said to St. Catherine of Sienna: "make yourself capacity, I will make myself torrent". Well, the way we are created makes of us "capacities of God" (see Catechism of the Catholic Church: nn° 27-49, "Man's Capacity for God").

## The Second Hidden Verse

The second commandment is stated as being "similar to the first" and has this clear affirmation: "love your neighbour as yourself". The "as yourself" poses another question: this means that God has already in one way, or another, asked us to "love ourselves"! It is a commandment of God to love ourselves! Of course, there are correct and upright ways of loving ourselves and wrong and sinful ways of loving ourselves! God is asking us to truly love ourselves, in a positive manner. Not only that, but He poses this love of

66

ourselves as a condition of becoming capable of loving our neighbour!

Here also there is a type of hidden verse between the two Commandments:

3- You shall love yourself in a truthful manner (hidden verse)

4- You shall love your neighbour as yourself.

**Suggestion:** if we receive God's love (the first hidden verse), if we are transformed by His love, we are indeed doing two things: we are loving ourselves, we are nourishing ourselves with Truth and Love! Since we are created in the image and likeness of God, God is our light and love, our nourishment, our happiness.
Some of us never thought that not only could we love ourselves, but also that this is a commandment, something we can't escape from! This is simply overwhelming!

## Conclusion

Indeed, the two main commandments are concealing deep surprises if we ponder on them.

Who wouldn't like to start his day by meditating and praying on the first hidden meaning, this mind-blowing overwhelming declaration of love from God: I am YHWH your God, and I do love you in an absolute, unconditional way: with all my heart, all my thought, all my strength: receive my love.

Why doesn't God declare his love for us from the very first pages of the Bible? Why when He gives the Law (the Ten Commandments) to Moses doesn't He state his love for us clearly, explicitly, before asking us to do the same for Him in return?

There is progressivity in the unveiling of His being! But, fundamentally, God's thirst, God's incredible love for each one of us is something hidden.

*"It is the glory of God to conceal a matter; to search out a matter is the glory of kings."* (Proverbs 25:2)

Searching out the matter is the glory of the human being! It is the meaning of his life. It is not curiosity or an ill habit! On the contrary, it is a fundamental aspect of human nature to dig and delve, to search, to try to find the secret, God's secrets!

*"it is the glory of God to conceal a matter"*! and truly He is hidden! We confess it every time we go to Mass: don't we say: *"heaven and earth are full of your glory"*? Do we really see God's glory on earth?

The Book of Wisdom says: *"Wisdom shouts in the streets. She cries out in the public square."* (Proverbs 1:20). Do we hear Wisdom's voice? She shouts in our streets! How come we don't hear her? Our earthbound ears are just not used to sound of her voice!

*"Give me Oh Lord the Wisdom who is seated at your side!"* (Wisdom 9:4)

# The Goal of Our Life is Union with Christ

**Question:** *"Union with Christ", can you deepen for me the reasons why this is the ideal answer? There are many answers that we can say or use, and our answers always fall short of the reality.*

*Jesus in St. John talks about "being one". St. Paul mentions "Christ living in me". "Died with Christ, risen with Christ," alludes to a deep union. Is "union" according to Tradition a preferred term? St. John of the Cross speaks about "Union of Love", and St. Teresa of Avila speaks more about "Spiritual Marriage".*

**Answer:** First and foremost, in order to give it a good answer, it is advisable to see what God says to us in the Scriptures. He is our guide, He knows us, and He knows what is best for us.

## Scriptures

It is true that when Jesus is praying to the Father in St. John's Gospel Chapter 17: 11, 21, 22, when just on the verge of starting his Passion and Redemption, He rather seems to be talking about "being one." St. Therese endorses it with the words: I prefer unity rather than union. "Union" implies there are still two of us while "unity" stresses we become one. This is correct, nobody can challenge this. However, if for the first time we are facing someone with the goal of our Christian life, the term "unity" could be a little too strong. Such a strong expression should not be used this early, as it could be a little confusing in the sense that the person can easily assume that if we become one with Jesus, He certainly will have absorbed their being, and therefore the question which would then arise is: what then happens to us? Do we disappear?

When we speak about union, we first of all find that it relates to human marriage. In fact, God describes human marriage in very strong terms: they become one… what God has united let not man put asunder. This is enforced by the way the man knows his wife and is something always expressed in very deep and stirring words. In this sense, the physical reality of marriage is the first union upon which we are invited to meditate and to contemplate, not under our own sensual categories or material ways, but adhering to God's ones. He is emphatic about this type of union. Not only this, but he underlines the fact that his union is not the union simply of two beings, but the union of two beings who are similar and who can act together as one. Therefore, when God is trying to find another creature to fill the loneliness of Adam, He searches for a creature who is similar with whom he can collaborate, work with, help, support and do the same things together. "The Lord God said, "It is not good for the man to be alone. I will make a *helper suitable* for him."" (Gen. 2:18)

One can notice the loneliness of Adam as being a very deep statement about God's state and God's desire to find us and be united to us. This is a very deep insight into God's Being. God is in search of a companion, face to face, somebody with whom He can interact face to face, can share the same breath, the same life – a companion pure and simple.

Moreover, this image of union or marriage is not used only once, it is constantly used in the Old Testament before even being used by Christ himself.

Thus in Hosea we have powerful expressions of love where God himself is the Groom and his People, Israel is the Bride.

*"Therefore I am now going to allure her; I will lead her into the wilderness and speak tenderly to her. 15There I will give her back her vineyards, and will make the Valley of Achor a a door of hope. There she will respond b as in the days of her youth, as in the day she came up out of Egypt. 16"In that day," declares the Lord, "you will call me 'my husband'; you will no longer call me 'my master.' 17 I will remove the names of the Baals from her lips; no longer will their names be invoked. 18 In that day I will make a covenant for them with the beasts of the field, the birds in the sky and the creatures that move along the ground. Bow and sword and battle I will abolish from the land, so that all may lie down in safety. 19 I will betroth you to me forever; I will betroth you in d righteousness and justice, in e love and compassion. 20 I will betroth you in faithfulness, and you will acknowledge the Lord."* (Hosea 2:14-20)

We can be constantly tempted to think that union or marriage is an image, a symbol, and nothing more, while in fact these amazing verses are open windows, allowing us to have a glimpse into the Devouring Fire who *is* God. He himself clearly states He is a Devouring Fire and that He is Jealous: who can understand these expressions when applied to God? Who can measure this divine thirst for us? For each one of us? Who can understand his Holy Name: Yahweh, which is a verb for "desire", a verb which expresses divine yearning? This is what constitutes his very nature!

71

The image of marriage, then, is repeated comes back again and again. We find it in Ezekiel where God uses Ezekiel as an example of God himself, of his loneliness, his betrayed or forgotten love: God deprives Ezekiel of his wife who dies. This is for us to reflect and ponder! We are his bride. What is our stance? Do we stand face to face before Him? His mirror-image, standing before of Him? Acknowledging Him as our partner? Or are we trying to find other partners?

Here again is how God will express his burning Fire, in marital terms, in nuptial terms:

*"1 The word of the Lord came to me: 2"Son of man, confront Jerusalem with her detestable practices 3 and say, 'This is what the Sovereign Lord says to Jerusalem: Your ancestry and birth were in the land of the Canaanites; your father was an Amorite and your mother a Hittite. 4 On the day you were born your cord was not cut, nor were you washed with water to make you clean, nor were you rubbed with salt or wrapped in cloths. 5 No one looked on you with pity or had compassion enough to do any of these things for you. Rather, you were thrown out into the open field, for on the day you were born you were despised. 6 " 'Then I passed by and saw you kicking about in your blood, and as you lay there in your blood I said to you, "Live!" 7 I made you grow like a plant of the field. You grew and developed and entered puberty. Your breasts had formed and your hair had grown, yet you were stark naked.*
*8 " 'Later I passed by, and when I looked at you and saw that you were old enough for love, I spread the corner of my garment over you and covered your naked body. I gave you my solemn oath and entered into a covenant with you, declares the Sovereign Lord, and you became mine.*
*9 " 'I bathed you with water and washed the blood from you and put ointments on you. 10 I clothed you with an embroidered*

*dress and put sandals of fine leather on you. I dressed you in fine linen and covered you with costly garments. 11 I adorned you with jewellery: I put bracelets on your arms and a necklace around your neck, 12 and I put a ring on your nose, earrings on your ears and a beautiful crown on your head. 13 So you were adorned with gold and silver; your clothes were of fine linen and costly fabric and embroidered cloth. Your food was honey, olive oil and the finest flour. You became very beautiful and rose to be a queen. 14And your fame spread among the nations on account of your beauty, because the splendour I had given you made your beauty perfect, declares the Sovereign Lord.*

*15 "But you trusted in your beauty and used your fame to become a prostitute. You lavished your favors on anyone who passed by and your beauty became his. 16 You took some of your garments to make gaudy high places, where you carried on your prostitution. You went to him, and he possessed your beauty. 17 You also took the fine jewellery I gave you, the jewellery made of my gold and silver, and you made for yourself male idols and engaged in prostitution with them. 18And you took your embroidered clothes to put on them, and you offered my oil and incense before them. 19Also the food I provided for you—the flour, olive oil and honey I gave you to eat—you offered as fragrant incense before them. That is what happened, declares the Sovereign Lord.*

*20" 'And you took your sons and daughters whom you bore to me and sacrificed them as food to the idols. Was your prostitution not enough? 21You slaughtered my children and sacrificed them to the idols. 22In all your detestable practices and your prostitution you did not remember the days of your youth, when you were naked and bare, kicking about in your blood."* (Eze. 16:1-22)

This, then, is followed by the entire book of the Song of Songs of Solomon: a marvellous description of the intimate love between

God (Jesus) and the Bride (Mary, the Church, each one of us). This is the "Holy of the Holies" of the knowledge and experience of God's Love, and Union.

In the New Testament, God takes on human nature, the human nature of a man, and He describes himself as the Groom. We can even consider some common texts and see how they open for us new avenues into the Lord's way of seeing his relationship with each one of us. When, for example, they asked Him if a man could divorce his wife, Jesus, the Groom, the *only* groom replies: "from the beginning it was not this way" (Mt. 19:8). Of course, on the surface He is talking about the relationship between man and woman. But at a deeper level, as we have seen above, the real Adam is Jesus himself. This is why He calls himself the "Groom" and the real woman is each one of us, hence leading to a deeper reading of Genesis 2. In this sense, then, we can also read the following: the human being was never meant to be separated from God.

Significantly then, why is Christian marriage indissoluble? Because of one reason only: it is instituted in the image of an indissoluble marriage, i.e. the marriage between Jesus and each one of us, between Jesus and the Church, between God and his people.

From these writings it is clear that the notion of union stays central throughout the Scriptures. Union relates to marriage and marriage is union. What God united, let not man put asunder. First and foremost, however, we must consider that we are talking about union, the marriage between the human being and God.
A further image can also be viewed, namely, the Wedding at Cana which is the first and the last sign that Jesus performs in St. John's Gospel.

It is indeed the first – at the forefront of the Signs St. John presents! Let us notice that on purpose we are deliberately not told who the Groom and the Bride are, because for St. John each one of Jesus' disciples is the bride and Jesus is the Groom! But first and foremost, Jesus' Mother is the main and essential bride. She is the New Eve, the Woman! This is the reason for her being called "woman" during Cana's Wedding because she is taken from Him, namely, she is the first one to come out of his side on the Cross, she is truly flesh of his flesh, bone of his bones! It is worthy of note, too, that this is also very Eucharistic ("this is my body…").

Of great interest is the fact that St. John starts the first of his examples with the nuptial sign and finishes with it, and also does the same in the Book of Revelation. In the latter this is found in the first vision even if not explicitly nuptial and in the last two chapters of the Book which describes the wedding of Jesus and his Bride. The entire book, in fact, is on the preparation for this wedding.

Again, at the foot of the Cross, the one who comes first from his opened side, Mary, his mother, is called again "woman". The New Adam, as we find is in Genesis 2, contemplates this amazing new being, and describes it by saying what he finds in her: the similarity, the total capacity for a companionship, i.e. for marriage and bearing children – she is flesh of my flesh, she comes from me, I can see this.

Deep mysteries to be thought on, indeed.

## Sacraments

Baptism is traditionally seen as a nuptial sacrament (see St. John Chrysostom's homilies on Baptism), where Jesus is the Groom and the baptised person is the Bride.

In addition, the essence of the Eucharist can be seen as nuptial. If in human marriage man and woman give everything to the other, here in the Eucharist Jesus gives us all his being: body, soul, spirit and divinity and much more, because Jesus has in Him all creation and all human beings. Both on the Cross, and in the Eucharist, Jesus does not keep anything for himself. All that He has He gives. This is even stronger than human marriage! In fact, human marriage is shaped in the image of the Marriage and Union of Jesus with each one of us and not vice versa! This leaves consecrated people who are betrothed to Jesus, in the "original" relationship, with the real Groom authentically married, and leaves married people only with a "photocopy" (so to speak) of the real Marriage. The consecrated have the real deal. This is why they are called Jesus' brides; this is why they dress for their solemn Profession as brides and sometimes wear a wedding ring. Returning to the Eucharist, moreover, we can see that because of its all-encompassing dimension, it must be seen as a Union, a Comm-union.

## Theology

If we look at the first part of last century's renewal in Spiritual Theology, the notion of union was very prominent. It is true that other expressions were also used, i.e. "perfection" "perfection of Love", "holiness", but of them all the notion of Union remains central.

St. John of the Cross uses "Union of Love" with Jesus as the Groom! One can contemplate his book "Spiritual Canticle" to see the most nuptial book ever written. It tells us the story of the development and growth of divine love between the human being who becomes the bride and is united with Jesus the Groom. The future bride, wounded by the fiery love of the Groom, goes out in search of Him and grows, is purified, transformed, prepared and adorned by the Holy Spirit and betrothed to the Groom, Jesus, in love.

"Union" is not the only expression, but it is still very probably the strongest and most evocative one, because human marriage is involved and is probably the strongest living image of the mystical love between Jesus and each one of us.

When the Doctors of Spiritual Life explain "union" to us they talk about two things: 1- the moment of fuller union with Christ, i.e. Spiritual Marriage, and that this means to them that the human being has entered a new state, 2- a state of Union. It is like marriage for when one marries, he or she not only is wed, but also starts a new life in this state and stays married and bears fruits to God.

## Human Desire

It is also quite common, with a great number of people from youth onwards, to want to find the love of their life, to love and be loved to the fullest extent! Often it is a natural desire in many, and equally often it is also repressed or disappointed or wounded through human experience. Isn't this deep genuine desire in us the hidden divine desire that God left in us, so that by his grace we can search for Him and find Him and finally find the one and only Groom – One who is human and divine at the same time? The fullness of love, the real Prince Charming. The fulfilment of all our desires to love and be loved. He is human, He can understand us, we can relate to Him! He is divine, God, therefore He can fill the infinite thirst we have in our heart to love and be loved. Isn't our heart created in His image and likeness? Aren't we all called to experience the passion of his fiery love? Aren't we all called to love Jesus with all our heart, all our soul, all our energy, all our mind? Why so? Because He loves us with all his heart, all his soul, all his energy, all his mind. Because He is the only one who can fill our infinite thirst to the brim.

He dares to ask us for everything because He wants to give us everything. To whoever gives Him everything, He shows a Royal Love like no other love on earth. He is not asking for half of our desire, half of our heart, half of our time! He is asking for everything! A Devouring Fire. A Divine Passion.

## Ministering Jesus' Love

The vocation of the minister of Jesus is to discover this love in himself and to experience the fullness of love itself. He is then sent by Jesus to show others the real Groom and how to fall in love with Him and experience the fullness of Jesus' love. Does he really have another mission?

This is what St. Paul means when he says the words "I betrothed you as a bride to Christ, namely, I am jealous as to you with the jealousy of God. For I have betrothed you to one husband, to present a pure virgin to Christ." (2 Co 11:2)
Do we need clearer words than this?

## Going Deeper: Jesus' Baptism, the Cross

If we deepen our understanding of Jesus' Baptism, if we try to put ourselves in his shoes so to speak, we will find that his main aim is to unite himself with us, not becoming a sinner like us, or having a fallen nature, but by transforming us into Him, bringing us to his light and love.

If we go deeper into his Baptism and his further baptism as He calls his Passion ("I have a baptism with which to be baptized, and how I am distressed until it should be accomplished!" (Luke 12:50)), we begin to understand that what He earnestly wants is to unite himself to each one of us. In fact, "baptism" is an

78

immersion, it tries as much as possible physically to mimic a deep transformation and union. He is baptised in us, He carries us. But also, from the beginning of His Passion He carries each one of us in Him and pulls us back to his light and love. This is the mystical operation of redemption. As the real Good Shepherd, He crosses the abyss that separates Him from us, searches for we, who are lost, in the darkness, and having found us He carries and supports us! Here starts the mystery of the mystical operation of Redemption: in fact, He proceeds, with the operation through the Holy Spirit, God's Charity and He unites his body with ours, his soul to ours, and his spirit and divinity to ours. In uniting us to Him He roots us in Him. This mystical operation He himself calls: Baptism: "I have a baptism with which to be baptised" (Luke 12:50), alluding to the Cross.

Like a sponge, his body absorbs, unites our body to his. His soul also, his spirit and divinity too. This is the result of what the Holy Spirit achieves between Jesus and us during the Passion and Crucifixion of the Lord. During this horrendous ordeal, during the six hours when He is suspended on the Cross, He seems fixed, not being able to move, but He is infinitely much more mobile than ever, with the mysterious operation of the immense love He has for us: the action of the Holy Spirit: "having loved his own who were in the world, He loved them to the end" (John 13:1). How did he love them to the end? First the Father entrusted all of us to Him, then He unites all of us to himself: "knowing that the Father has given Him all things into his hands" (John 13:3). We are in the darkness, we became darkness because of our separation from God, because of our sins. Yet, despite this God the Father gives us into his hands! What a mystical undertaking!

# God is Much Better Than You Believe

Here below we have a letter from St. Therese of the Child Jesus to her sister Leonie. Her understanding of who is God, what pleases Him is simply mind-blowing.

### LT 191 From Therese to Leonie.

J.M.J.T.

Jesus                                                July 12, 1896

Dear little Leonie,

I would have answered your charming letter last Sunday if it had been given to me. But we are five, and you know I am the littlest... so I run the risk of not seeing the letters until after the others or else not at all... 1 saw your letter only on Friday, and so, dear little sister, I am not late through my own fault... If you only knew how happy I am to see you in these good dispositions...

I am not surprised that the thought of death is sweet to you since you no longer hold on to anything on earth. I assure you that God is much better than you believe. He is content with a glance, a sigh of love... As for me, I find perfection very easy to practice because I have understood it is a matter of taking hold of Jesus by His Heart. ... Look at a little child who has just annoyed his mother by flying into a temper or by disobeying her. If he hides away in a corner in a sulky mood and if he cries in fear of being punished, his mamma will not pardon him, certainly, not his fault. But if he comes to her, holding out his little arms, smiling, and saying: "Kiss me, I will not do it again," will his mother be able not to press him to her heart tenderly and forget his childish mischief?... However, she knows her dear little one will do it again on the next occasion, but this does not matter; if he takes her again by her heart, he will not be punished...

At the time of the law of fear, before the coming of Our Lord, the Prophet Isaias already said, speaking in the name of the King of heaven: "Can a mother forget her child?... Well! even if a mother were to forget her child, I myself will never forget you." What a delightful promise! Ah! we who are living in the law of love, how can we not profit by the loving advances our Spouse is making to us... how can we fear Him who allows Himself to be enchained by a hair fluttering on our neck.

Let us understand, then, how to hold Him prisoner, this God who becomes the beggar of our love. When telling us that it is a hair that can effect this prodigy, He is showing us that the smallest actions done out of love are the ones which charm His Heart.

Ah! if we had to do great things, how much we would have to be pitied?... But how fortunate we are since Jesus allows Himself to be enchained by the smallest things...

It is not little sacrifices you lack, dear Léonie, is not your life made up of them?.. 1 take delight at seeing you before such a treasure and especially when thinking you know how to profit from it, not only for yourself, but for souls... It is so sweet to help Jesus by our light sacrifices, to help Him save souls that He bought at the price of His Blood and that are awaiting only our help in order not to fall into the abyss...

It seems to me that if our sacrifices are the hairs which captivate Jesus, our joys are also; for this, it suffices not to center in on a selfish happiness but to offer our Spouse the little joys He is sowing on the path of life to charm our souls and raise them to Himself...

I intended writing Aunt today, but I have no time; this will be on next Sunday. 1 beg you to tell her how much I love her and dear Uncle as well. I am thinking very often of Jeanne and Francis.

You ask me for some news about my health. Well! dear little sister, I am not coughing anymore. Are you satisfied?... This will not prevent God from taking me when He wills; since I am putting forth all my efforts to be a very little child, I have no preparations to make. Jesus Himself will have to pay the expenses of the journey and the cost of entering heaven....
Adieu, dear little sister, I love you I believe more and more....

Your little sister, **Thérèse of the Child Jesus** rel. carm. ind.

Sister Genevieve is very happy with your letter; she will answer you the next time. All five of us kiss you....

# Christ the Groom, What Does it Mean?

**Question:** Some people criticise the spousal language that St. Teresa of Avila uses when she is speaking to Christ. An example of this from the 16ᵗʰcentury Teresa of Avila, a Doctor of the Church, occurs before her death when she exclaims: *"O my God, my Spouse, finally I shall see You!"* My question is: is there any foundation, both in the Scriptures and the Early Church, for the use of spousal language when speaking to God?

**Answer:** Not many Catholics are familiar with this dimension. It is not the only way many female consecrated saints see the Lord, but it is an important dimension. In general, only people called to live such a relationship with Christ understand it. As Jesus puts it in the Gospel: not many understand this language, only the person who is given it (see Matthew 9:11)! Otherwise, I am tempted to say, they wouldn't marry, and would seek this love in a total dedication to Jesus. Indeed, a special grace is needed to understand it. Even if one hears about it and sees it in Scriptures and in Tradition, two major difficulties or obstacles remain which can stop us from understanding or accepting it.

First, one must understand that even if the language is very audacious it must be understood in purity, without involving any genitality. Some people are so trapped in their sensuality or so filled with Freudian psychoanalysis, that they can't reach the purity of understanding that it is possible to love the Lord purely, in a nuptial way, without involving any sensuality or sexuality or genitality. This is the first obstacle to overcome.

Now, the second obstacle, regards heterosexual men: imagine if they admit that such a thing existed, what can they get from it? While it is easier for a woman than for a man to love Jesus with purity and spiritually as the Groom, for a heterosexual man, instinctively, it looks far beyond his reach.

Does this exist in the Scripture? Without a doubt, for in the Gospel Jesus is called "the Groom" various times. The problem is that the majority of people see it as symbolic. Sadly, this also applies to the imagery used for nuns when they consecrate themselves and are called "Jesus' Bride". People still think that it is rather symbolic; they don't take it seriously. St. Paul says that the betrothed is like a virgin to Christ: "For I am jealous as to you with the jealousy of God. For I have betrothed you to one husband, to present a pure virgin to Christ." (2 Co 11:2).

In addition, in the Old Testament an amazing secret book can be found – the *Song of Songs*. It describes a love relationship between a man and a woman, Solomon and his bride. Again, here too people take these images symbolically, instead of realistically, because they struggle to believe for the two above-mentioned reasons. The Christian Traditional interpretation says that the Groom in this book is Jesus, and the bride can be Mary, the Church, and the Soul. Also look at the beautiful and powerful passages of Hosea 2, and Ezekiel 16 where God expresses his jealous love for his people.

Now the Theological Tradition mentions it too, regarding the Sacrament of Baptism. St. John Chrysostom comments at length on Baptism and he sees it as St. Paul did in the quotation above, i.e. as a nuptial sacrament where we are betrothed to Christ who is the Groom. Consequently, therefore, the Baptised person wears a white alb, representing the wedding dress.

Because of the above-mentioned difficulties, you do not often hear about this dimension understood as a real loving relationship with Jesus the Groom. Even among priests and theologians it is rare to find it truly understood and believed. It is rather something that stays as the "secret" of the nuns. Of course, there are no secrets but since it is still a delicate matter, it tends to be referred to in hushed tones rather than proclaimed out loud.

Now the question is: is this real? Well, yes, the female saints talk to us about it and show it to us. Why not believe them? St. Agnes, Martyr, gently rejected a proposal of marriage because she wanted to stay a virgin and pure for Jesus. St. Catherine of Alexandria received from the heavenly Groom a mysterious ring – the nuptial ring. This is well known. If some people don't want to see it, or can't psychologically see it, this is totally acceptable for, again, one needs a very special grace to view it from this perspective.

I personally totally believe in this and even consider it as central in the way we entrust ourselves to God. Notice that the first commandment doesn't consider our capacity to love, and that it should be divided into two parts: the divine part, which is addressed to God and the human part, which normally goes to the husband or wife, who can fill it. No. He says: you shall love me with *all* your heart! ALL... so, even the love that we think we can and should give to a human should, is to God. Our heart is created in the image and likeness of God, not of a human being. Therefore, our being is capable, because of how God made it, of fully loving God himself and only God can fill it properly and totally.

Does this mean that we are not supposed to ever marry? No, this means that the sacrament of Marriage is based on a previous sacrament, the sacrament of Baptism. And that the sacrament of Baptism is the sacrament where we are betrothed to the Lord, where we give Him all our heart! Once our heart is given to Him totally, and experiences how He can love us and fill our heart even humanly (not involving anything genital), then we are enabled to love in a true way and marry sacramentally. Of course, this is the ideal, but nothing stops us from aiming toward the real ideal and the real Groom, Jesus.

Even more significant is the fact that a husband will rarely die for his wife. Look at Jesus, He gave his Body, his Soul, his Spirit, and his Divinity and died for each one of us. Doesn't this make of Him the real Groom? In Catholic Theology we define the Sacrament of Marriage as the mutual gift of oneself between a particular man and woman. The total and unique gift of oneself. Isn't this realised by Jesus himself, totally and perfectly?

Receiving Communion, too, is in fact the mutual gift of ourselves. God and we are each entrusting his entire being to the other. He gives himself to us totally when the Priest offers us Holy Communion. We say "Amen", but are we not then supposed to give ourselves to Him? In this sense, this sacrament is fully nuptial.

**"This is a hard teaching. Who can accept it?"** (John 6:60)
We can't deny that saying that "Jesus is really the Groom" constitutes a major difficulty for heterosexual men.

Nobody, however, addresses this issue in a satisfactory way. People say: – ok, there is Our Lady. While in fact Our Lady is not

God, only Jesus is. Mary is not the bride of the Christian. She is not God. She can't fulfil the criteria. In this sense, emotionally, the heart of Christian men, and of consecrated men, stays empty. Why? Because a heterosexual man can't easily relate to Christ as the Groom. He can't *fall in love* with Him, as the Groom.

If the heart and the emotions are not fulfilled and transformed, however, can there be proper Christian chastity?

More to the point, if a man hasn't experienced Jesus' love as the Groom, can he really preach Christ?

We hear different replies and explanations to this major difficulty: some say that there are different ways to see Jesus, and that Jesus-The-Groom is not the only one. Point taken. But the heart and the emotions of a man remain unfulfilled, unrealised.

There must be a solution for this serious problem. The core of the problem is that real holy chastity is in the heart first. Therefore, if the heart is not filled by this nuptial love, the desire for nuptial love will remain unfulfilled.

Others will say: the Community one serves takes the place of the Bride to love. This is not wrong, but this occurs at a later stage of development and growth, after "Jesus-The-Groom" has first been discovered.

As you can see, we try, we try, we repeatedly try to find answers, but they are false, or better said: they come from a good will but in reality, are incomplete, and therefore unsatisfactory.

The heart of a consecrated man, the heart of a Priest, is supposed to be filled with this unique love of Jesus. But he is a man. And if he is heterosexual (attracted to women only) how can he fall in love with another man? God chose to become incarnate in the human nature of a man, not a woman. Admittedly St. Paul says that there are no differences between men and women. Easily said than done, by contrast, when it comes to emotions, desire, desire to love and be loved.

In sum, therefore, half of our heart, so to speak, remains not given to anybody and very thirsty.

This is a serious issue! And strangely, everybody seems to be escaping from it. But on the contrary, there is a solution to this huge dilemma! Let us look at it closely.

In each one of us there is a feminine and a masculine side, regardless of our biological and psychological gender. This truth can, sometimes, be hard to take in, especially by heterosexual men in certain cultures. But it is a fact. A deep psychology fact and a spiritual fact. This of course doesn't go against the fact that in each gender, the major traits and personality remain "genderised". A man bears inside of him a feminine and a masculine side, but his body/biology and his psychology, his personality, are a man's. It is not because we have both sides deep in us that our gender or appearance, or psychology become hazy, buoyant, or undetermined. A man stays a man even if he discovers that he has a feminine side inside of him, and a woman stays a woman even if she has a masculine side inside of her.

In a human being, too, the total person and the feminine/masculine sides in the person are not of the same category/dimension and proportion. The Person is "genderised". A man has male traits, the psychology of a male, the biology of a male. The same is true for a woman. But inside of each one of them, there are these feminine/masculine sides: they are like entities, part of the whole. The part is not the whole.

Are these feminine and masculine sides in us developed, transformed, and fulfilled? Being created in the image and likeness of God means, that not only can He speak to and fulfil these two areas in us, but it means that He offers us role models, so to speak, for each one of them, examples of their fulfilments, in order to allow them to grow, develop and reach full realisation. In order to discover ourselves better, let us not lose sight of Jesus Our God and Saviour, the Groom, but keep Him as the goal and centre of our life. He is our everything, fully man and fully God. A Unique being. One Person. He is *the* Groom; He is supposed to be loved also with all our emotions. Let us focus, then, on the disciple who follows Jesus, who is supposed to be loved and love Jesus. This disciple is what interests us. How can we become really and fully His disciples? How can we fulfil and realise all our being, masculine and feminine?

**Note:** There are two forms of love: *Eros* and *Agape* (please see Pope Benedict's Encyclical letter: "God is Love"). Our erotic capacity to love (our *eros*) needs an object to love and who can return the needed love. This divine love then will elevate this capacity, transform it and purify it. Jesus' Love for us makes our *Eros* become *Agape* – being capable of loving in an oblative way, Jesus in us loving our neighbour.

## The Feminine Side

Let us start by addressing the feminine side as God presents it to us, in a role model. Let us remember that these so called "sides" (feminine and masculine) are not the whole person but deep aspects or parts of our being. They have their existence in our soul, functioning, acting and developing therein. They develop our attitudes, insights, perceptions and virtues.

In whom (and where) in the Gospel is femininity embodied to the maximum? This question is asked in a specific way: "to the

91

maximum of perfection, according to God". Because we have many other examples and moments in the Gospel or in the Bible of excellence, we need to maximise the most perfect and emblematic example.

The answer is: Mary in the Annunciation. There we find her in a receptive silence; she listens; she enters into a personal relationship with God and she is invited to receive life within her and take care of it, to which she offers herself and commits totally. Can Mary be here the role model of men and women? Yes. Would a heterosexual man have difficulty to make this prayer to God: "God, give me a heart like Mary's in the Annunciation so I can listen to you and put what you say to me into practice, offer myself totally"? Absolutely not. Would he feel that something about his masculinity is taken away or diminished or changed? On the contrary, if he looks carefully, deeply inside himself, he will find that in this case, if he received a new heart like Mary's one, he would become more of a human being (more authentically human and humane), more real, more complete. Let us say, in other words: he is developing his feminine side, according to God's plan of creation and redemption.

## The Masculine Side

Now, let us move on to the masculine side: Who (and where) in the Gospel embodies masculinity to its maximum? It is true that we can find many examples of masculinity in the Bible. But here again the question is to find it present to the maximum of perfection, and not just any masculinity. Paradoxically here also the person is the same: Mary. Where? At the foot of the Cross. The strongest person on earth the most resilient, (she is standing), with the most powerful capacity to forgive, is Mary at the foot of the Cross and during the hours which follow. Peter who said he would defend Jesus and die for him, showed his "masculine" side here to be an utter disaster. The power of virtue, by contrast, manifests itself in the most shining way in Mary at the foot of the Cross. Who can equal her? Who has this power and strength?

## True Masculinity Comes from True Femininity

Now, let us notice that true masculinity blossoms and develops from true femininity and not the other way around. Peter, with a false masculinity, tried to be strong declaring that he would fight and die for his Master; his femininity was obviously not yet fully developed. He had not yet discovered Mary in the Annunciation as a role model. His masculinity was artificial, "machista" so to speak. He needed to discover Mary, her strength, but also to discover from where true strength came, and allow Mary to grow in him.

What a lesson is revealed here for both men and women. Mary starts the journey of our development and Mary shows us to which extent of transformation and virtue God can go and realise in us.

## Mary *the* True Bride

In order to start the journey of transformation, Mary, we can now see, is the starting point. She shows us in the Annunciation how to listen to Jesus' Word, how to be receptive to it, how to develop this "feminine side" in us. How to fall in love with Jesus. Jesus is Her God and Her Saviour; she loves Him also as the true and only bride of the God incarnate. In it because He is her God and her Saviour He can also be considered as her true Groom! We need to be careful here. These apparently human aspects should be taken in a pure, true, and divine way.

Mary herself is the true bride. There are no other brides. It is in Mary that we can fall in love with Jesus, allowing Mary the only Bride, to grow in us and through her to enter into a love relationship with Jesus.

93

Again, this is valid for both men and women. Our feminine side and our masculine side are led by Mary the true Disciple and the true Bride. She shows us the way to realise our being. She offers to our erotic capacity to love a way to be touched by Jesus' Love, to grow, develop and reach its fullness. It is under her leadership, moulded and transformed by the Holy Spirit so that we can really and truly become the true Bride, love and be loved by Jesus the Groom.

There is nothing wrong for a man, during the Prayer of the Heart, to allow Mary in Him to love Jesus as a true Virgin, a true Bride. There is nothing wrong, on the contrary, to allow Mary to grow, develop, under the power of Jesus' Love. This way, not only female saints love Jesus, but also male saints can do so in Truth and in Spirit.

### Discovering and Receiving *The* Groom's Utter Love

To reiterate: God says to us, *"You shall love the Lord your God with all your heart, and with all your soul, and with all your mind."* (Dt 6:5). Jesus is God. Jesus is Our Saviour, and He loved each one of us in a unique way and died for each one of us, giving himself to each one of us totally. In this sense, we can hear the first commandment coming from Jesus who is our God and our Saviour: *"You shall love me, your God and Saviour, with all your heart, and with all your soul, and with all your mind".*

He does not say: "love me with *part* of your heart. No. *All* of your heart should be involved! Not only the part of your heart that you give to God, but also this part of your heart that you, mistakenly, give to a human being – the lower half of your heart. Mary in the Annunciation didn't leave out this part of her heart when she said to me: YES, here I am."

Again, we can hear the first commandment said truly from above the Cross: *"I am your God and Saviour, I am your Groom, you shall love me with all the capacity and energy and desire of your heart.* You can't leave some desire to love and be loved unfulfilled. By being God and man, being your everything, I can fill this desire that I myself put in you to love and be loved. Look at my saints who discovered this and lived it. – St. Therese of the Child Jesus, St. Teresa of Avila, and thousands of others."

We need to hear Jesus the Groom saying: *"I Love you with all my heart, and with all my soul, and with all my mind.... In the Eucharist, I give you all my heart, all my emotions, all my love, all my desire to love you and be loved by you".*
This is the Truth.

# The Act of Oblation
### (The best way to receive God's Love)

### Introduction to the
### ACT OF OBLATION TO MERCIFUL LOVE
### From the Autobiography of saint Thérèse of the Child
### Jesus Ms A

"This year June 9, [1895] the feast of the Most Holy Trinity, I received the grace to understand more than ever before how much Jesus desires to be loved.

I was thinking about the souls who offer themselves as victims of God's Justice in order to turn away the punishments reserved to sinners, drawing them upon themselves. This offering seemed great and very generous to me, but I was far from feeling attracted to making it.

From the depths of my heart, I cried out: 'O my God! will Your Justice alone find souls willing to immolate themselves as victims? Does not Your Merciful Love need them too?

On every side this love is unknown, rejected; those hearts upon whom You would lavish it turn to creatures, seeking happiness from them with their miserable affection; they do this instead of

97

throwing themselves into Your arms and of accepting Your infinite Love. O my God! Is Your disdained Love going to remain closed up within Your Heart? It seems to me that if You were to find souls offering themselves as victims of holocaust to Your Love, You would consume them rapidly; it seems to me, too, that You would be happy not to hold back the waves of infinite tenderness within You. If Your Justice loves to release itself, this Justice which extends only over the earth, how much more does Your Merciful Love desire to set souls on fire, since Your Mercy reaches to the heavens. O my Jesus, let me be this happy victim; consume Your holocaust with the fire of Your Divine Love.'"

You permitted me, dear Mother, to offer myself in this way to God, and you know the rivers or rather the oceans of graces that flooded my soul. Ah! since the happy day, it seems to me that Love penetrates and surrounds me, that at each moment this Merciful Love renews me, purifying my soul and leaving no trace of sin within it, and [84v°] I need have no fear of purgatory. I know that of myself I would not merit even to enter that place of expiation since only holy souls can have entrance there, but I also know that the Fire of Love is more sanctifying than is the fire of purgatory. I know that Jesus cannot desire useless sufferings for us, and that He would not inspire the longings I feel unless He wanted to grant them.

Oh! how sweet is the way of Love! How I want to apply myself to doing the will of God always with the greatest self-surrender! Here, dear Mother, is all I can tell you about the life of your little Thérèse; you know better than I do what she is and what Jesus has done for her. You will forgive me for having abridged my religious life so much.

How will this "story of a little white flower" come to an end? Perhaps the little flower will be plucked in her youthful freshness or else transplanted to other shores. I don't know, but what I am certain about is that God's Mercy will accompany her always, that it will never cease blessing the dear Mother who offered her to Jesus; she will rejoice eternally at being one of the flowers of her crown. And with this dear Mother she will sing eternally the new canticle of Love.

––––––

## ACT OF OBLATION TO MERCIFUL LOVE
## J.M.J.T.

### Offering of myself as a Victim of Holocaust to God's Merciful Love

O My God! Most Blessed Trinity, I desire to Love You and make You Loved, to work for the glory of Holy Church by saving souls on earth and liberating those suffering in purgatory. I desire to accomplish Your will perfectly and to reach the degree of glory You have prepared for me in Your Kingdom. I desire, in a word, to be a saint, but I feel my helplessness and I beg You, O my God! to be Yourself my Sanctity!

Since You loved me so much as to give me Your only Son as my Saviour and my Spouse, the infinite treasures of His merits are mine. I offer them to You with gladness, begging You to look upon me only in the Face of Jesus and in His heart burning with Love.

I offer You, too, all the merits of the saints (in heaven and on earth), their acts of Love, and those of the holy angels. Finally, I offer You, O Blessed Trinity! the Love and merits of the Blessed Virgin, my dear Mother. It is to her I abandon my offering, begging her to present it to You. Her Divine Son, my Beloved Spouse, told us in the days of His mortal life: "Whatsoever you ask the Father in my name he will give it to you!" I am certain,

99

then, that You will grant my desires; I know, O my God! that the more You want to give, the more You make us desire. I feel in my heart immense desires and it is with confidence I ask You to come and take possession of my soul. Ah! I cannot receive Holy Communion as often as I desire, but, Lord, are You not all-powerful? Remain in me as in a tabernacle and never separate Yourself from Your little victim.

I want to console You for the ingratitude of the wicked, and I beg of You to take away my freedom to displease You. If through weakness I sometimes fall, may Your Divine Glance cleanse my soul immediately, consuming all my imperfections like the fire that transforms everything into itself.

I thank You, O my God! for all the graces You have granted me, especially the grace of making me pass through the crucible of suffering. It is with joy I shall contemplate You on the Last Day carrying the sceptre of Your Cross. Since You deigned to give me a share in this very precious Cross, I hope in heaven to resemble You and to see shining in my glorified body the sacred stigmata of Your Passion.

After earth's Exile, I hope to go and enjoy You in the Fatherland, but I do not want to lay up merits for heaven. I want to work for Your Love alone with the one purpose of pleasing You, consoling Your Sacred Heart, and saving souls who will love You eternally. In the evening of this life, I shall appear before You with empty hands, for I do not ask You, Lord, to count my works. All our justice is stained in Your eyes. I wish, then, to be clothed in Your own Justice and to receive from Your Love the eternal possession of Yourself. I want no other Throne, no other Crown but You, my Beloved!

Time is nothing in Your eyes, and a single day is like a thousand years. You can, then, in one instant prepare me to appear before You.

In order to live in one single act of perfect Love, I OFFER MYSELF AS A VICTIM OF HOLOCAUST TO YOUR MERCIFUL LOVE, asking You to consume me incessantly, allowing the waves of infinite tenderness shut up within You to overflow into my soul, and that thus I may become a martyr of Your Love, O my God!

May this martyrdom, after having prepared me to appear before You, finally cause me to die and may my soul take its flight without any delay into the eternal embrace of Your Merciful Love. I want, O my Beloved, at each beat of my heart to renew this offering to You an infinite number of times, until the shadows having disappeared I may be able to tell You of my Love in an Eternal Face to Face!

Marie, Francoise, Therese of the Child Jesus and the Holy Face, unworthy Carmelite religious.
This 9th day of June, Feast of the Most Holy Trinity, In the year of grace, 1895.

**Note:** The underlined part is indulgenced.

---

**Question 1:** What is the full significance of the word 'oblation'? What is it trying to capture? What is its full meaning? Is it "offering up your heart"? I would love for you to expand on this!

**Answer:** 'oblation' here is the translation of the French 'offrande'. Thérèse could have used the french word 'oblation'. She preferred 'offrande'. 'Offrande' is 'to offer', 'offering', which is: giving. She'll rightly define the act of love this way: 'to love is to give everything and to give oneself to God'. You see, she very easily switched from 'offering' to 'giving'.

Since God created us and created us free, this means that:
1- We are free
2- We possess ourselves

God chooses not to possess us. This is why and how we can love: we have something we can give…

Remember, the definition of the Sacrament of Marriage: the mutual gift of each of the parties (the Groom and the Bride). 'Mutual git of': this is love: each one gives himself (as a gift) to the other one.

God possesses everything, except us, human beings, created 'at His Image and Likeness'. He doesn't need us to offer Him what He already possesses. The dearest being on earth for God is the Human being, but He doesn't possess him. He left him free, free to love or not, to give himself or not. He can't force the human being to love Him.

We do own the dearest thing in the eyes of God, the thing that pleases Him the most: ourselves. Offering Him the only 'thing' He doesn't have pleases Him enormously!

The very act of offering ourselves is an act of Love.

**Now, another question might rise:** what is to 'offer ourselves'?

**Answer:** Let me give you a first example to open the way: sometimes we can worry a lot about an issue, ok? We feel, and know that we are 'carrying that problem in us'. It can be very heavy indeed, even though it is in the soul. And then, while we are praying, God comes and asks us to 'entrust' Him that problem. We feel that it requires from us an act of detachment. It might cost us a lot to do this inner act, because we do possess a lot our problems. Then, we reach the point where we end up by offering, entrusting, putting in His Hands the Problem.

Well in this case it was a problem that we were offering. Now imagine all ourselves, our past, present, future, our body, soul, spirit, all what we possess, all what we are, all our richness, talents, the graces received. They are not 'problems' but they are elements to which we could be attached to. And God knows how it might cost sometimes to offer ourselves to Him. Sure, one can very easily admit that in order to do so, we need to things:

1- to know Him a little bit more than just a superficial knowledge of God, it requires a bit of experience of Him.

2- a big trust in Him, and trust comes from experiencing His overwhelming love.

**Question 2:** Well, it made me think of two things:

1. In the Mass, when we are invited to "Lift up our hearts to the Lord" (you have mentioned this part of the Mass before). I understand that the Mass is an oblation, an offering, but would this part of the Mass be reminding us of/ and our opportunity to practice our oblation to God?
2. It made me think of "prayer of the heart" – could this be seen a kind of oblation/offering up our hearts?

**Answer:** Definitely the Mass in an oblation/offering. During the Mass, we offer ourselves to God, as God offers/gives Himself to us. Definitely 'lift up your heart' is a reminder for us to offer ourselves. Without hesitation, I would consider all these acts being exactly the same: to love – to offer ourselves – to lift our heart to Jesus (seated at the right Hand of the Father) – the Prayer of the heart.

The base of all is in fact the 'power' we receive in Baptism to offer ourselves to God: the priesthood of the faithful. We are united to Him, this is why He gives us a share in His Priesthood. We can then, as priests in Christ, offer ourselves to God, and offer Christ to the Father. We can offer our brothers and sisters, the entire world to God.

All the faithful are invited to participate [spiritually] to the Mass. In order to do so, they have to exercise their priesthood (not to be mixed with the Priesthood of Ordained Ministers).

An offering presupposes:

   1- A Priest (that offers, elevates),
   2- An Altar (the leaning point),
   3- A Victim (to offer)
   4- A Fire (to burn, elevate, transform).

In Christ-Priest we are priests. The Altar is Christ himself as well. His capacity, in the Trinity (He is at the Right hand of the Father), to offer, direct the offering to the Father. He is the rock, the fulcrum. The Victim here to offer is ourselves. The Fire is the Holy Spirit, the Merciful Love of God.

You find here all our way to enter in the Mass, especially its second part ('lift up your heart'), the Offertory where, with the bread and wine, we offer all our life to God, and later as well, in Jesus, the Host, we offer ourselves to the Father in the Fire of the Holy Spirit. Remember in the Third Eucharistic prayer we have: 'May He [the Holy Spirit] make of us an eternal offering to you".

The Prayer of the Heart, is that same exercise of lifting up our heart (as saint Paul invites us to do, or Jesus by saying: 'dwell in me'), but repeated gently, extended in a period of time. But it should become our final destination. This is when we are united to Jesus in 'spiritual marriage'.

**Question 3:** Also, St Therese refers to the oblation as "one single act of perfect love": ¡SEP¡ "In order to live in one single act of perfect Love, I offer myself as a victim of holocaust to your merciful Love, asking you to consume me incessantly…"
What do you think she means by "one single act" and this act being an act of "perfect love"? Do we too need to offer ourselves up as "victims of the holocaust of love" in order to enter into this single act of perfect love?

**Answer:** This is an obvious double question that one asks when he/she reads Thérèse's Act: what is "one single act" and what is "perfect love".

I was just saying, above, that we should extend the time of dwelling in Christ. Remember the offering means that He comes and takes us and immerses us in Him. So as a result, we dwell in Him. And dwelling in Him (one, two, three minutes, or sometimes, an hour or more, it depends on Him and on our degree of transformation in Him)…. means that He outpours the Holy Spirit in us. This is why it is of the utmost importance to practice the prayer of the heart: we allow God to give himself to us, transforming us in Him.

"one single act", one single active act… she wants to remain in Him, active, as much as possible. Yes, 'Love attracts our love'. I would rather say: a heart beating style of "single act". In the sense that it is not a simple passive position, it is a burning position, and, even if it is long lasting, it has a form of a heart beating. Remember saint Paul speaks about the "movements" of the Holy

Spirit deep in us saying: "the Spirit Himself intercedes for us with unspoken groaning" (Romans 8:26). The "groaning" is repetitive. So it is not static but dynamic.

I would then say that we start by not having it 'one continuous active immersion in Jesus' (one single act). We come out of the immersion, so we do repeat the act of offering. Day after day, we grow spiritually, we are transformed in Him, then we are invited to reach that hight of a "continuous act" or "one act".

The act of 'pure love': I would be here more prudent. I would consider the "pure act of love" as the act that fulfils the conditions mentioned above (Priest, Victim, Fire, Altar..), and the most important one is to lean on Jesus himself only, on His merits as Thérèse takes time to explain in the long long introduction to the Act of Oblation (all what precedes the last paragraph of the specific act of offering). This means that we need to have the "Altar" (and not to lean on ourselves), and the Power of the Holy Spirit (not our capacity of lifting in the air (not in the water)).

Let me here show you another passage where she explains it:

"A scholar has said: "Give me a lever and a, fulcrum and I will lift the world.". What Archimedes was not able to obtain, for his request was not directed by God and was only made from a material viewpoint, the saints have obtained [36 v] in all its fullness. The Almighty has given them as fulcrum: HIMSELF ALONE; as lever: PRAYER which bums with a fire of love. And it is in this way that they have lifted the world; it is in this way that the saints still militant lift it, and that, until the end of time, the saints to come will lift it." (End of Manuscript C)

Of course, you might argue: – she is not speaking of the Prayer of the Heart, but the prayer of intercession. – Well, no, it is absolutely the same. And they are both about lifting. "a soul that is burning with love cannot remain inactive" reminds us Thérèse. Therefore, the more Charity grows in us, the more God entrusts us automatically more brothers and sisters. Therefore, the Prayer of the heart becomes a power apostolic weapon of conquest. (we might come back to this apostolic aspect of the Prayer of the heart)

**Now your last question:** "Do we too need to offer ourselves up as "victims of the holocaust of love" in order to enter into this single act of perfect love?"

**Answer:** It is like asking me: is it necessary to practice the "Prayer of the heart" in order to reach that "single act of perfect love"? Well yes, it helps, because of the outpouring of the Holy Spirit that happens during that time of immersion in God. But it is not the only means. It is one leg, the other is Lectio Divina, the proof of love: 'if one loves Me, he will put into practices my commandments' (John 14:23).

**Note:** Regarding *Lectio Divina*, please read the book: "Lectio Divina at the School of Mary", Jean Khoury.

———————————

### Letter 197
### From Thérèse to Sister Marie of the Sacred Heart
### J.M.J.T. Jesus

#### September 17, 1896

Dear Sister, I am not embarrassed in answering you… How can you ask me if it is possible for you to love God as I love Him?…If you had understood the story of my little bird, you would not have asked me this question. My desires of martyrdom are nothing; they are not what give me the unlimited confidence that I feel in my heart. They are, to tell the truth, the spiritual riches that render one unjust, when one rests in them with complacence and when one believes they are something great. ... These desires are a consolation that Jesus grants at times to weak souls like mine (and these souls are numerous), but when He does not give this consolation, it is a grace of privilege. Recall those words of Father: "The martyrs suffered with joy, and the King of Martyrs suffered with sadness." Yes, Jesus said: "Father, let this chalice pass away from me." Dear Sister, how can you say after this that my desires are the sign of my love?... Ah! I really feel that it is not this at all that pleases God in my little soul; what pleases Him is that He sees me loving my littleness and my poverty, the blind hope that I have in His mercy.... That is my only treasure, dear Godmother, why would this treasure not be yours?... Are you not ready to suffer all that God will desire? I really know that you are ready; therefore, if you want to feel joy, to have an attraction for suffering, it is your consolation that you are seeking, since when we love a thing the pain disappears. I assure you, if we were to go to martyrdom together in the dispositions we are in now, you would have great merit, and I would have none at all, unless Jesus was pleased to change my dispositions. Oh, dear Sister, I beg you, understand your little girl, understand that to love Jesus, to be His victim of love, the weaker one is, without desires or virtues, the more suited one is for the workings of this consuming and transforming Love. ... The desire alone to be a victim suffices, but we must consent to remain always poor and without strength, and this is the difficulty, for: "The truly poor in spirit, where do we find him? You must look for him from afar," said the psalmist. ... He does not say that you must look for him among great souls, but "from afar," that is to say in lowliness, in nothingness.... Ah! let us remain then very far from all that sparkles, let us love our littleness, let us love to feel nothing, then we shall be poor in spirit, and Jesus will come to look for us, and however far we may be, He will transform us in flames of love....Oh! how I would like to be able to make you understand what I feel!... It is confidence and nothing but confidence that must lead us to Love.... Does not fear lead to Justice (1)?... Since we see the way, let us run together. Yes, I feel it, Jesus wills to give us the same graces, He wills to give us His heaven gratuitously. "Oh, dear little Sister, if you do not understand me, it is because you are too great a soul.. .or rather it is because I am explaining myself poorly, for I am sure that God would not give you the desire to be POSSESSED by Him, by His Merciful Love if He were not reserving this favour for you.. .or rather He has already given it to you, since you have given yourself to Him, since you desire to be consumed by Him, and since God never gives desires that He cannot realize. ...Nine o'clock is ringing, and I am obliged to leave you.' Ah, how I would like to tell you things, but Jesus is going to make you feel all that I cannot write....I love you with all the tenderness of my GRATEFUL little childlike heart. Thérèse of the Child Jesus rel. carm. ind.(1) To strict justice such as it is portrayed for sinners, but no this Justice that Jesus will have toward those who love Him.

---

**Question:** If we are not to petition during the Prayer of the Heart (PH) and Lectio Divina (LD), when and how should intercessory prayer happen/take place?

**Answer:** As an allocated moment (time and space), intercessory prayer should happen at a special time, as a specific type of prayer. During Mass we have a time for it, as we do during the Divine Office (I am sure that in our personal prayer as well we do pray for others).

Your may ask the same question for other types of prayer as well: Prayer of Praise and Prayer of Thanksgiving, "when shall we say them?".

Here I would like to explain more clearly the deep relationship between LD & PH on the one hand and Intercessory Prayer on the other.

It is important to remember that LD is a key unavoidable type of prayer today. It is by far the most transformative type of prayer. Why? Because it allows a part of Christ (today's part of Christ-Word Bread) to become incarnated in us and transform us in Him. The more we are transformed in Christ the more powerful our intercession becomes (acts on God). Jesus explains the relationship between Lectio Divina and the efficiency of our prayer (which has been answered) in the Gospel of St John where He says: if you do my Will (keep my commandments) ask me all what you want (because you'll BE in my Name) and you will receive it, i.e. the Father will grant it to you (see John 15:7). If LD is done properly, all its transformative power will be enacted. Then PH becomes much more fruitful and even more transformative. Otherwise, if you practise PH without LD, its transformative power is dramatically decreased.

Now let us consider what happens during the PH. While we are practising the PH, the Power of the Holy Spirit is working in our depths and through us will help Lift the entire World to God the Father in the Son, through the Holy Spirit. This is done automatically. The more we are transformed in Jesus, the better it works – automatically. St Therese explains that wonderfully at the end of her Manuscript C, in the Story of the Soul.

She says:
"All the saints have understood this, and more especially those who filled the world with the light of the Gospel teachings. Was it not in prayer that St. Paul, St. Augustine, St. John of the Cross, St. Thomas Aquinas, St. Francis, St. Dominic, and so many other famous Friends of God have drawn out this divine science which delights the greatest geniuses? A scholar has said: "Give me a lever and a fulcrum and I will lift the world." What Archimedes

110

was not able to obtain, for his request was not directed by God and was only made from a material viewpoint, the saints have obtained in all its fullness. The Almighty has given them as fulcrum: HIMSELF ALONE; as lever: PRAYER which burns with a fire of love. And it is in this way that they have lifted the world; it is in this way that the saints still militant lift it, and that, until the end of time, the saints to come will lift it."

Intercessory prayer has different levels of power and action. What is more powerful than to pray for somebody or – if it was given to you by the grace of God – to take this person and lift him/her to God and introduce him/her into God's Fire of Love? Here St Therese presents to us the most powerful version of Intercessory Prayer.

It is a duty of love for us to pray for everybody. St Paul says that we have to pray for one another all the time, without excluding any other person. St James in the end of his Letter, mentioning the Prophet Elijah speaks about the power of a prayer that is heard/answered by God. This should grab our attention and invite us to deepen our understanding of Intercessory Prayer.

In addition, one has to remember the relationship between Intercessory Prayer and the Priesthood of the Faithful. A Priest "prays for" others, like St Paul invites us to do all the time. (This is why we have the Divine Office. But it is something that becomes second nature to us, it is part of the "fabric" of the New Creature that we become in Christ. Being "in Christ" makes the Fire of the Holy Spirit that dwells in Him, pray in us and through us. The Holy Spirit knows how to pray and knows what we should ask for, and the way God wants it. What depends on us is not to pay attention to all that multiplicity of things to pray for. Our duty is just to get closer and closer to Jesus and to the Fire of His Love and be transformed by IT.

St Therese developed those important questions in two different places in that same Manuscript C, in the Story of the Soul:

"Since I have two brothers and my little Sisters, the novices, if I wanted to ask for each soul what each one needed and go into detail about it, the days would not be long enough and I fear I would forget something important. For simple souls there must be no complicated ways; as I am of their number, one morning during my thanksgiving, Jesus gave me a simple means of accomplishing my mission.

He made me [34r°] understand these words of the Canticle of Canticles: "DRAW ME, WE SHALL RUN after you in the odour of your ointments." O Jesus, it is not even necessary to say: "When drawing me, draw the souls whom I love!" This simple statement: "Draw me" suffices; I understand, Lord, that when a soul allows herself to be captivated by the odour of your ointments, she cannot run alone, all the souls whom she loves follow in her train; this is done without constraint, without effort, it is a natural consequence of her attraction for You. Just as a torrent, throwing itself with impetuosity into the ocean, drags after it everything it encounters in its passage, in the same way, O Jesus, the soul who plunges into the shoreless ocean of Your Love, draws with her all the treasures she possesses. Lord, You know it, I have no other treasures than the souls it has pleased You to unite to mine; it is You who entrusted these treasures to me, and so I dare to borrow the words You addressed to the heavenly Father, the last night which saw You on our earth as a traveller and a mortal. Jesus, I do not know when my exile will be ended; more than one night will still see me singing Your Mercies in this exile, but for me will finally come the last night, and then I want to be able to say to You, O my God:

"I have glorified you on earth; I have finished the work you gave me to do. And now do you, Father, glorify me with yourself, with the glory I had with you before the world existed.

"I have manifested your name to those whom you have given me out of the world. They were yours, and you have given them to me, and they have kept your word. Now they have learned that whatever you have given me is from you; because the words you have given me, I have given to them. And they have received them, and have known of a truth that I came from you, and they have believed that you sent me.

"I pray for them, not for the world do I pray, but for those whom you have given me, because they are yours; and all things that are mine are yours, and yours are mine; and I am glorified in them. And I am no longer in the world, and I am coming to you. Holy Father, keep in your name those whom you have given to me.

"But now I am coming to you; and these things I speak in the world, in order that they may have joy made full in themselves. I have given them your word; and the world has hated them, because they are not of the world, even as I am not of the world. I do not pray that you take them out of the world, but that you keep them from evil. They are not of the world, even as I am not of the world.

"Yet not for these only do I pray, but for those who through their word are to believe in me.

"Father, I will that where I am, these also whom you have given me may be with me, that they may see my glory which you have given me, because you loved me from the foundation of the world. And I have made known your name to them, and will make it known, that the love with which you loved me may be in them, and I in them.'"" (Manuscript C)

In fact, Thérèse is explaining the Common Priesthood of the Faithful, received in Baptism, in Jesus-Priest. And a few pages afterwards she gives a further explanation of her new way of praying, her new way of practising the Prayer of the Heart:

"Mother, I think it is necessary to give a few more explanations on the passage in the Canticle of Canticles: "Draw me, we shall run," for what I wanted to say appears to me little understood. "No man can come after me, unless the FATHER who sent me draw him," Jesus has said. Again, through beautiful parables, and often even without using this means so well known to the people, He teaches us that it is enough to knock and it will be opened, to seek in order to find, and to hold out one's hand humbly to receive what is asked for. He also says that everything we ask the Father in His name, He will grant it. No doubt, it is because of this teaching that the Holy Spirit, before Jesus' birth, dictated this prophetic prayer: "Draw me, we shall run.""

What is it then to ask to be "Drawn" if not to be united in an intimate way to the object which captivates our heart? If fire and iron had the use of reason, and if the latter said to the other: "Draw me," would it not prove that it desires to be identified with the fire in such a way that the fire penetrate [36r°] and drink it up with its burning substance and seem to become one with it? Dear Mother, this is my prayer. I ask Jesus to draw me into the flames of His love, to unite me so closely to Him that He live and act in me. I feel that the more the fire of love burns within my heart, the more I shall say: "Draw me," the more also the souls who will approach me (poor little piece of iron, useless if I withdraw from the divine furnace), the more these souls will run swiftly in the odor of the ointments of their Beloved, for a soul that is burning with love cannot remain inactive. No doubt, she will remain at Jesus' feet as did Mary Magdalene, and she will listen to His sweet and burning words. Appearing to do nothing, she will give much more than Martha who torments herself with many things and wants her sister to imitate her." (Manuscript C)

All that Thérèse is describing happens in the same movement of the Prayer of the Heart. Jesus attaches people to us (without us doing it or knowing it), so when we do the PH we perform, as well, our Priestly duty of intercession. In the Prayer of the Heart we offer our being to Jesus and are immersed in Him. The more we are transformed in Jesus the more we are like a sponge, unknowingly absorbing all the persons Jesus wants us to carry. They are like our mystical body ("Union with Jesus" is union with a portion of his Body). So whenever we do the Prayer of the Heart (The more we are transformed in Jesus, the more PH becomes more and more constant in us), and we are then immersed (with them) in His Fire. The Power of the Holy Spirit in us is lifting not only us but all our mystical body.

[Many more things occur during the PH, and this is just to reply to your question and show the deeper levels of Intercession and their relationship with our level/degree of transformation in Jesus and with the practice of the PH.]

In conclusion we can say that it is not really possible to separate deep powerful intercession from our being, from our PH. When somebody asks us to pray for him/her, or we just remember to pray for a certain person/intention, let us not forget that (in my eyes) the most powerful, perfect and pure way to do it is to entrust this intention to Our Lady, by saying one "Hail Mary" and that's it. If your remember again this person/intention, you may just redo that again: say the "Hail Mary", entrusting this person to Mary. St Therese used to say that Our Lady knows better the will of God (what to say to God and how to say it), we don't. In this sense she is called "Throne of Wisdom", because the Wisdom of God, Jesus, is dwelling in her in His absolute perfection while it is not the case for us. We either carry too much the person, or worry too much, or are busy too much in dealing and arranging the life of others, forgetting our utter ignorance. And all this is not intercessory prayer, but impurity added to our way of dealing with God.

The following book is linked to this chapter: Jean Khoury, "Mary's Fiery Prayer".

# Therese's Copernican Revolution

After having been seriously warned by God of the importance of St. Thérèse, right after her death and for various decades, to the point that one of the Popes said that she is "the greatest saint of modern times", interest tended to fade until a point was reached where Thérèse is back in the normal ranks of the saints.

In itself it would be a deep loss for the Church to lose sight of the paramount importance of Therese for the institution itself. Some will argue by saying that St. Faustina's message is the same as Therese's. Others will argue that the fact that Pope John-Paul II declared her a "Doctor of the Church" goes against what I am saying. These two arguments may seem strong but when you look at the reality, on a daily basis, Therese is not being understood as God wanted her to be understood during the decades following her death. Others might argue by saying: "has she ever really been understood even in the past?", or "weren't we loyal to the gentle Little Flower of Lisieux and still haven't reached the core of her teaching and the meaning of her mission in the Church?". When Mgr. Guy Gaucher OCD was interviewed in 1992 – the year of the publication of all her works in one volume – and after her Doctorate in 1997 – he declared: "everything is starting now"! Here he meant that the adventure of knowing the real Therese was just starting! A hundred years after her death!

Therese is just not any saint. She is unique in the history of the Church; she is well above other saints. I can hear people already being upset when they read this. But this statement is not said lightly. In the history of the Church, in the two thousand years of our trying to understand the Gospel and trying to live it, Therese is unique. In the two thousand years of spiritual masters in the Church, Therese is different, but not slightly different, she is "revolutionarily" different and well above the crowd of the

117

Masters of Spiritual Life. However, instead of arguing, it is better to try to understand why such statements are being made. I do not claim that this article will give all the reasons, but some of them are set out below:

1. Her extremely deep and developed relationship with Our Lady which is totally overlooked. We fix on stereotypes, quoting some of her writings and neglecting the main body of her writings. We don't really see who she is in relation to Our Lady.
2. Her capacity to embody the deepest teaching in Spiritual Life we have today, ie. as expounded by St. John of the Cross.
3. The practical discernment she offers on living St. John of the Cross' teaching, without any extraordinary manifestations... what she calls "the common way" (la voie commune). This way still embodies a deep mystical/spiritual life which reaches the summits of spiritual life.
4. Her practical spirit, which reveals how to love Jesus on a daily basis, using all the events of the day to love Him, and the notion of martyrdom by pinpricks.
5. Her first trial (1889-1892) and its significant import.
6. Her Act of oblation which sheds an incredible light on the Spiritual Life, on prayer, and on contemplative prayer, and also on how we manage our relationship with God.
7. Her hope and conviction that God wants to give her all that she has read about in St. John of the Cross.
8. Her "Little Way" so often misunderstood.
9. Her final trial (1896-1897) and its profound meaning... the list is long and in all these fields and topics, she offered incredible new lights.
10. Her way of praying for others, and realising to its fullness the baptismal priesthood, reaches incredible depths and shows forth many lights.

11. The radically different face of God she shows us. Her experience and knowledge of God is of another league. The same applies to her understanding of the Gospel and the Scriptures.
12. The way she deals with God directly: a mix of incredible audacity, deep understanding of who God really is, how He thinks, how He sees us, etc. How she deals with Him in a daily and practical way.
13. Of course, and the most important point is the way she loved Jesus. This it must be said includes all the above.

The Icon of Therese Doctor of the Church

## Therese's Copernican Revolution

There is yet one more important revolutionary insight she offers about our relationship with the Lord, that is, our relationship with the Holy Spirit. On the one hand this can sometimes be overlooked, while on the other hand it can free, or unblock, many people on their spiritual journey. The insight I am referring to combines all the elements above. In order, then, to explain her insight, I think we can summarise it under three aspects which should be combined and blended spiritually:

**1-** Who we are, our weaknesses, our past sins, the deep stains of sin in us, the bad habits, our faults....

**2-** Who God is, His true face or identity – here Therese is simply mind-blowing – how He looks at us; what He expects from us; what He would like to do in us; His incredible desire to give Himself to us.

**3-** The conditions needed for us to love God. They are not what we think, for example, when we feel we need to please Him by doing good deeds. What to do with our weaknesses, how to deal with our sins (after having sinned), how to love God, how to become holy despite or because of our weaknesses... how to open our being – regardless of our state (sins, faults, etc) – to God's unconditional Love.

Therese enters the Carmelite monastery of Lisieux at the age of fifteen years. At the age of seventeen she reads St. John of the Cross, the *Spiritual Canticle* and the *Living Flame*, and asks God to realise is her all that she has read. She undergoes a deep purification, through difficult, increasingly purifying trials, from 1889 to 1892. As a result of God's action in her, she learns from within about her own nothingness. After this spiritual winter, from 1893 onward, she enters a new spring phase where the love of God is guiding her.

The sequence of events that follow amply reveals how this new phase unfolds.

On 9th Jun 1895 she receives a very powerful grace showing her to what extent God's desire to love us goes, in order to give us his love: the Holy Spirit (she names Him: the Merciful Love of God).

She understands that her lack of holiness, in that all her righteous deeds have stains on them, so they would fail to please God anyway, is not the obstacle to God's outpouring of Love, but that the contrary is true – **this is a huge discovery where the dynamics of our relationship with God are turned upside down**. She then feels invited to offer herself totally, unconditionally (as a holocaust offering) to God's merciful love. From that moment onward until her death she is on fire in a completely new way. In April 1896 she is introduced by God to the "land of the shadow of death" (Is. 9:2), to sit "at the table of the sinners," just like Jesus who wanted to sit and eat with sinners (Mt. 9:11), and she prays with her brothers and sister sinners to be forgiven and set free. The inner Fire is still there but not felt anymore, as will become clear from Letter 197 (see below). In September 1896 she experiences an important retreat. She gives a written account of this retreat to her sister Marie who lives with her in the Monastery. Her account is a prolongation of the new dynamics decisively triggered by the Act of Oblation. In fact, she offers more details and development of the Act. This text is called today the Manuscript B. In reply to the account of her retreat, her sister Marie objects to her saying that she is much weaker than Therese, not on fire like her, that she doesn't feel any passion of love like her, and more importantly and as a consequence Marie feels she cannot offer herself to God's love, that she is unworthy, etc. In a word she says: "I am not like you," to which Therese replies with a fiery letter, Letter 197, see below. In this letter, Therese develops what can be already perceived during her first trial (1889-1992) and which was hugely reinforced on 9th June 1895. The doctrine she offers – we must call it a "doctrine" – is here revolutionary, almost unheard of in the history of the Church. It is an illustration and development of something we read in St. Paul, but which we fail to really grasp to the core. St. Paul writes: "He [the Lord] said to me: 'My grace is sufficient for you, for my power is made perfect in weakness.' Therefore, I will boast all the more gladly about my weaknesses, so that Christ's power may

121

rest on me." (2 Cor. 12:9) We think of perfection in a certain way, as if it were an eradication of all weaknesses, of being strong when faced with trials and temptations, of having overcame all possibility of falling, only to discover that God's understanding of the perfection of love, is something completely different. It is rather the case that the more we rely on His Love the more His love is active in us. Our weakness is not an obstacle, if we learn to offer it to God's love. Our perfection is, in all truth, God's love in us.

But first let us re-read this letter (please see previous chapter).

The usual understanding of Spiritual Life is that our sins displease God, therefore, we need to repent, refrain, confess, and change. We think we first need to be perfect in order to please God. All these dynamics, however, are measured by our way of "measuring" sin or "good deeds". Significantly, we look at ourselves instead of looking at God. We think that we can please God. We don't have any doubt about that, and we think it is through avoiding sin that we can please God. Of course, this is correct: under no circumstance should we sin. We clearly need to avoid sin. But the problem lies elsewhere: we think that this is what makes us please God and be accepted by Him. We think that we *can* please God, that it is in our power to do so. The point is that, yes, it is necessary to please God, but these dynamics are not enough. The core of Therese's discovery on the 9th June 1895, is that even our "good" acts have stains in them (see Act of Oblation). Even our righteous acts have stains on them. This means that we can't, by our own efforts, please God – we need something else, we need another way. In fact, **we need God to please God**, because only God (in us) can please God. It is as if we are in a closed circuit. And we need to enter this circuit.

How does this work? First and foremost, one has to admit that this discovery is proper to an advanced stage in spiritual life. But

Therese wasn't shy about sharing it with everyone. In fact, from day one it shows the way to the beginner. She even called it "her own little way to God, direct and easy", compared to the hard staircase of holiness. In fact, the hard staircase of holiness is an allusion to asceticism, to our own efforts made with the general help of the Grace of God. But, per se, there are *no* hard staircases which really lead to holiness. It is just an illusion that the majority of we humans have – we think that we can be good Christians by our own efforts, by our own codes of conduct and morals. But in fact, without the Holy Spirit (the Merciful Love of God) we can't please God. We need to receive the Holy Spirit, allow Him to "grab" our inner being, as it is, transform it, elevate it and introduce it to God himself. We need the Holy Spirit to became capable of pleasing God.

The main objection seems to cling to us still: "I am weak, a wretch, I have greatly sinned, I keep falling, for me, it is impossible to please God" …. "I don't feel God's love".… It would never occur to us – and this is Therese's Revolution – that the weaker we are, the more we are adapted to God's Love. God's weight, God's desire is to lower Himself more and more! God, says Therese, finds a greater satisfaction in lowering Himself more. Thus, our weakness is not an obstacle but an advantage, with the important conditions of accepting it, and offering it. We never think that God waits for us to offer our weakness, even our sin. We want to offer the good things in us to God. We don't know that our being is combustible to God's Love. Anything in us, if offered with trust and abandonment, is combustible for the Fire of God's Love.

What is good in us is not enough in the eyes of God: all our righteous deeds have stains. This means we can't please God with our righteousness. We need to offer to the Holy Spirit even what we thought in the past was "good". He takes it, penetrates it, transforms it, elevates it and introduces it to God. He makes it

123

pleasant to the eyes of God. Therefore, anything in us, good or less good or God forbid, bad, needs to be offered to God's love. Anything and everything in us is really combustible to the Fire of God's Love.

Remember, God is a real Fire, a Fire which doesn't destroy, but gives divine life, makes us become alive, active, loving.

In this sense what was thought to be an obstacle – our weakness, sinfulness etc. – can be used as something combustible to God's Fire of Love in us. Our "excuses" are now our assets. It depends on we ourselves to use them.

We hear Jesus saying: I came for the sinners so they can have divine life! I didn't come to ask them to be holy and then I can receive them. I came to change them, I came to give them my Love, which can transform them, make them pleasant to me, so that I can introduce them in Me.

In sum, then, instead of looking at ourselves in the spiritual mirror to see how "good" or "bad" we are, it is better to look at Jesus, see in his heart his desires to give us his Fiery Love. After sinning, it is important to look at Jesus, not at ourselves, which, sadly, sometimes seems to reinforce the sin by yet another sin, which is to delay the reception of Jesus' Merciful Love.
Lord Jesus, keep our eyes fixated on your Love, help us understand to which extent it is only your love which makes us pleasant to your eyes and introduces us deeply in you. Amen.

Lord Jesus help us see that the more we feel we are weak the more adapted we become to your love. Teach us O Lord to dwell in this spiritual poverty. Blessed are the poor in spirit, for theirs is Jesus' Fiery Love.

Please remember that the Prayer of the Heart, or Contemplative Prayer, is the best way to receive God's Love. To learn to practice it, don't hesitate to read the "Small Catechism of the Prayer of the Heart", or contact www.schoolofmary.org

Printed in Great Britain
by Amazon

36101618R00069